Conten

Crest Books and Colonel Phil Needham are pleased to provide *He Who Laughed First: Delighting in a Holy God* to Beacon Hill Press of Kansas City. We pray that the publisher's ministry, combined with that of The Salvation Army, will be strengthened by the message of this book. Crest Books is the publishing imprint of The Salvation Army National Headquarters, 615 Slaters Lane, Alexandria, Virginia.

I wish to thank those who have helped me bring this book to its completion. First is my wife, Keitha, who has endured my early risings for this work and served as both encourager and critic. Others who have offered helpful criticism are my good friend David Purdum, and Bruce Nuffer and Jonathan Wright of Beacon Hill Press of Kansas City. I am also grateful to Marlene Chase, editor in chief and national literary secretary for The Salvation Army in the USA, for her considerable encouragement and facilitation in enabling me to bring this project to publication. Whatever defects this book may have, however, are mine alone, not theirs.

I express particular gratitude to Dora Ramsay and Donalee Price for their assistance with clerical details and word processing.

Above all else, I am grateful to God for the sheer privilege and pleasure of crafting words for His glory.

HE WHO LAUGHED
FIRST

Delighting in a Holy God

Phil Needham

Beacon Hill Press of Kansas City
Kansas City, Missouri

Copyright 2000
by Beacon Hill Press of Kansas City

ISBN 083-411-8726

Printed in the
United States of America

Cover Design: Ted Ferguson

Library of Congress Cataloging-in-Publication Data

Needham, Phil, 1940-
    He who laughed first : delighting in a holy God / Phil Needham.
       p. cm.
    Includes bibliographical references.
    ISBN 0-8341-1872-6
    1. Joy—Religious aspects—Christianity. I. Title.

BV4647.J68 N44 2000
230—dc21

99-058946

10   9   8   7   6   5   4   3   2   1

Introduction

The Christian saint is hilarious.
—Tertullian

It took me a long time to hear God laughing. But then I began hearing some intriguing things. For one, I noticed the words of that time-honored confession of faith, the Westminster Shorter Catechism, concerning a Christian's "chief end" being "to enjoy Him forever." Now how do you enjoy someone who can't laugh? For another thing, I began to see more laughter in the Bible. It was mostly a matter of letting texts come alive, which in many instances revealed God's humor and the sheer pleasure of life with Him. And for yet another observation: the Christians I found myself most drawn to were those whose love for God had a fresh sparkle and whose outlook had generous doses of humor. Their holiness was a joyful attraction.

All of this led me to take God's humor seriously and to realize that it invariably affected people who were in love with Him. I am deeply in love with the human being I spend more time with than anyone else, my wife. The fact that she finds humor in situations that few can and expends enormous energy on laughter affects me deeply. It keeps me off balance in a good sort of way and lures me into becoming, hopefully, a more enjoyable person than I would otherwise have been. I have a deep suspicion—indeed, it has become my conviction—that in a similar way the humor of God rubs off on His saints, and His laughter resonates with the righteous.

This is why Tertullian, an early Church father, was right: the Christian saint *is* hilarious. He or she is sufficiently infected with God to join His laughter. The saint's God-given insight into life helps him or her see humor in new places. This marks the believer, frankly, as a humorous oddball in a world gripped by the pervasive sadness of self-absorption.

In this book I invite the reader to explore with me the hilarious side of holy living.[1] I think there are a few things about holiness that need to be set straight, things that have given it a bad reputation. Let's briefly describe what's wrong.

LAUGHING SAINTS

Holiness has frequently been claimed by, and associated with, perfectionists who lacked humanity, worriers who were obsessed with their imperfections, or pretenders who could not laugh at themselves. Legalists and lovers of rules have taken the call to holiness and made it into a very unattractive employ. Many people, Christians and non-Christians alike, have become so repulsed by those who very self-consciously strive after moral superiority that they often apply to them the phrase "holier than thou" to expose the real motivation: one-upmanship. It is also true, however, that such an accusation sometimes masks the accuser's own discomfort in the presence of a genuine saint, one whose character probes the sensitive spots of his or her own spiritual failure and serves as a reminder of who he or she was meant to be. For various reasons, therefore, holiness has all too often been associated with something beyond our grasp, undesirable, artificially enforced, or insufferably dull, and those who pursue it as exceptional or abnormal at best, and questionably motivated at worst.

No opinions could be further from Christian truth. Holiness was never intended to be the private domain of a spiritually elite; it is the privilege and call of all Christ's disciples. And when truly understood and lived, it is anything but dull. The life to which the Scriptures point is suffused with good cheer, childlike delight, and a certain carefree attitude. Perhaps this is the side of the story less known or told. But it needs to be. That's what we'll endeavor to tell in this book.

GOSPEL JOY

At the very heart of this understanding of holiness is the gospel itself. The New Testament message is a frontal assault on sadness and grim piety, and it offers a remedy for sinking despair. From the very beginning of the salvation story to its end, joy emerges again and again. The birth of the Savior brings joy (Luke 2:8-20); His message and ministry elicit joy in the people (Mark 12:37); near the end of His life He tells His disciples that the reason He has taught them is so that His joy might be in them and their own joy might be complete (John 15:11); having met their resurrected Lord, the disciples are overwhelmed with joy (Luke 24:52); the Early Church enjoys its life together (Acts 2:43-47); and the mission of the Church brings joy both to the recipients (8:8) and to the missioners (13:52). The New Testament dances with joy from beginning to end, and the message is clear: so should life. The gospel gives no support to a life that dwells in sadness. It not only calls us to a new way of life named holiness but also suffuses our lives with joy.

This is not to say that holiness is an easy road. For starters, it means taking up one's cross and dying to oneself (Mark 8:34-36; Gal. 2:19-20). It's for those who are ready to lay down their lives. But this does not mean that it's an enterprise for self-preoccupied high achievers and humorless holy types always weighed down with the burden of their goodness. On the contrary, it's for those who can accept easy yokes and light burdens (Matt. 11:30). It's for those who accept the help of Jesus. It's for those who some-how, incredibly, find strength in the midst of their weakness (2 Cor. 12:10). As much as the following pages will say about the hi-larious side of holiness, none of it should be construed to suggest a softening of the call to self-denial, to lose ourselves completely in God, so that we can live the life Jesus came to give.

Nor should it be construed to suggest that tragic, and even horrible, things do not happen to God's beloved disciples. They sometimes do. We are not spared jarring loss and painful grief. The joy of the Lord is not immunity to "the slings and arrows of outrageous fortune." It's not a guarantee of perpetual happiness. Rather, it's something deep enough to sustain us through tragedy, a joy that neither person nor circumstance can rob us of. It's something that marks us unmistakably as saints of God who know joy beyond joy.

In some ways this book reflects my own personal faith jour-ney into joy, a journey that I pray you can connect with in a helpful way. I hope readers who are overly serious types like me will find some liberating help in these pages. And I hope that those who are blessed with joy will come even more to appreci-ate the value of their gift, both to the world and to the Church, and the closeness of their humor to their holiness.

IMAGE OF GOD

The book begins with the hilarity of God (Part 1).[2] Hilarity on earth (Part 2) and in the Church (Part 3) means nothing if there's no hilarity in heaven. If God's not laughing, we can't laugh, for at our best we reflect His image.

As you read this book, keep in your mind that thought about being in His image. Holiness is the recovery of that image, lost through sin, and the holy life is its polishing toward perfection. Some would say that hilarity is out of place in such an atmosphere. I disagree. Hilarity fits perfectly.

But don't take my word for it yet. Keep reading.

Part 1

Hilarity
in Heaven

1

Creation Joy

It's important to recognize that hilarity begins in heaven. God created it. That's why the Bible sometimes depicts God as rejoicing and having a good time.

THE CREATOR AT PLAY

At the very beginning of Scripture, where the act of creation unfolds, we see a God who seems as much at play as He is at work. Of course, creating the universe is hard work, and even God chooses to rest for a day after six days of explosive creativity (Gen. 2:2). But as you read the account in the first chapter of Genesis, you get the impression that what God is doing here is fun.

Picture children at play. They're wholly wrapped up in what they're doing. They're serious about their fun. One of them says, "Let's do this!" The rest agree, and off they go. After they have enjoyed creating that particular imaginary world for a while, another one says, "I know what we can do—let's . . ." and off they go again, imagining into existence yet another scenario in which to play.

To me, that first chapter of Genesis has a similar feel to it. I imagine the threesome God[1] having a meeting with himself and saying, "Let's make light!" And He does. He quite likes what He's done and decides to separate this light from the darkness, creating two entities, which He names "day" and "night." There's no stopping Him now; His imagination is in full gear! He says, "Let's make a dome to separate the waters above from the waters below!" He does, and He calls it "sky." Now He's really on a roll! Next He separates the water below from the land, calling them "sea" and "earth." Then He creates the plants and trees on a third day and the sun and moon on a fourth. (Strange sequence, isn't it? You would think He would make the sun first so that the plants and trees had everything they needed to grow when they were created.) The next day it is the creatures of the sea and the birds of the air, followed the next day by the land creatures. All the while God is thoroughly enjoying himself and affirming the sheer goodness of the world He is calling into being out of nothing.

And then He raises the stakes. He decides to stick His neck out and create something more like himself: "Let us make humankind in our image, according to our likeness; and let them have dominion" (Gen. 1:26). He makes us. He calls us out of nothingness, molds us in His image, loves us as His own, and in this love gives us freedom. Then He steps back to admire the fruit of His creativity, all the while realizing that its crowning achievement, the human race, is the biggest risk creativity has ever taken. Knowing it could backfire, He has created the real possibility of love. A rush of excitement overcomes Him. He has enjoyed both the act and the outcome, with all the risks involved. He is pleased. "This is good," He says.

It seems to me, then, that even though creating a universe was a very serious and tiring business, the Lord had an extraordinarily good time of it. You also get this impression from Prov. 8:30-31. Robert C. Morris says that translators have sometimes struggled with translating these verses, perhaps because the original Hebrew is not at all solemn, not at all "adult." This passage describes God's creative wisdom at work in Creation—only, the image is not that of someone hard at work; it's that of child's play, of dancing before God. Here is Morris's translation:

> I was by God's side, a master craftsman,
>> delighting him day after day,
>>> ever at play before God's face,
>>>> at play everywhere in God's world,
>>>>> sporting with the children of earth.[2]

Can you picture the scene? Can you imagine God having such a good time watching His wisdom call forth splendor?

We need to come to terms with the fact that God takes delight in His creation. And no one has the potential to bring Him more joy than does the crown of His creation, "for the LORD takes pleasure in his people" (Ps. 149:4). He enjoys us.

NEW CREATION

In fact, God enjoys us so much that He's unwilling to allow our rebellion against Him to close the doors to joy. In Christ we can be led back to Him, or as the writer to the Hebrews says, "Enter the sanctuary by the blood [the total self-giving] of Jesus, by the new and living way that he opened for us" (10:19-20). This provision had been anticipated centuries before, and its final outcome nowhere more eloquently and enthusiastically expressed than by the prophet Isaiah: "I am about to create new heavens and a new earth; the former things shall not be remembered or come to mind. But be glad and rejoice forever in what I am creating; for I am about to create Jerusalem as a joy, and its people as a delight. I will rejoice in Jerusalem, and delight in my people" (65:17-19).

Alongside God's sadness over our sin is His joy over the new creation He is bringing about, and the joy will prevail because sin will die and the new creation will come to full fruition. He will even take a botched human creation, like the city called Jerusalem, and remake it into something delightful.

CREATION ENJOYED

God enjoys what He creates. He enjoyed it at the beginning, and He is enjoying its restoration and renewal. So should we. It is our nature to do so—our *true* nature. God's work is there for our enjoyment, and for a use that enhances human life without destroying the enjoyment. The psalmist speaks of the "givenness" of creation, of creation as part of the reliable order that God has created,[3] of "trees planted by streams of water, which yield their fruit in its season, and their leaves do not wither. In all that they do, they prosper" (1:3).

He invites us to delight in the trustworthy law of the Lord (1:4) and in the glory of our Creator's work: "O LORD, our Sovereign, how majestic is your name in all the earth!" (8:9). Creation is something for us to sing about.

In fact, the Bible says that creation itself joins in the fun. "The heavens are telling the glory of God; and the firmament proclaims his handiwork" (Ps. 19:1). God makes "the gateways of the morning and the evening shout for joy" (65:8). The meadows and the valleys "shout and sing together for joy" (v. 13). The sun "runs its course with joy" (19:5). When the Lord is ready to come, "the wilderness and the dry land shall be glad, the desert shall rejoice and blossom; like the crocus it shall blossom abundantly, and rejoice with joy and singing" (Isa. 35:1-2).

God will not allow the disaster of humanity's rebellion to thwart His purpose in creation. A confident invitation is extended to the universe: "Let the heavens be glad, and let the earth rejoice; let the sea roar, and all that fills it; let the field exult, and everything in it. Then shall all the trees of the forest sing for joy before the LORD; for he is coming" (Ps. 96:11-13).

It's only right that God's creation rejoice in His handiwork and in the promise of His providential care over it. The whole universe dances to the music of heaven, and God invites us to join in on the fun.

2

God's Laughter

It may be difficult to imagine a laughing God, but if there is joy in heaven, someone is laughing. It must be God.

LAUGHTER AND TEARS IN HEAVEN

What is this laughter of God? Mostly it is the sheer enjoyment of His own Persons. Remember: there are three of Him! His laughter, echoing across the universe, defines fun for us. It teaches us the enjoyment for which we are destined in Christ, where God makes His home among His children, dwells in their midst as their God, and wipes away every tear from their eyes (Rev. 21:3-4). It points the way to eternity. When God laughs, we know something is right.

Conversely, when He cries, something's wrong. The sadness of God has to do with one thing and one thing only: our sin. The Bible does not spare us the heart-wrenching story of a God who is broken by that sin. Beginning with the account of betrayal in the Garden (Gen. 3), there follows the ugly saga of sadness upon sadness as His people pursue false delights, a saga that reaches powerful poignancy in the story of the grief and hurt of Hosea, whose wife abandons him to pursue false lovers, a man who represents the God we have abandoned. This God grieves our lost estate in sin, then takes the form of a Man, and in that Man is revealed God's sadness over a people who refuse to return, a sadness that wept over a faithless Jerusalem doomed to destruction (Luke 19:41-44). Our sin grieves God.

It grieves Him because He chooses to be vulnerable to those whom He loves. He lets us get to His heart and even break it. If He truly loves us, He must allow us to hurt Him.

Nevertheless, we cannot take away His laughter. His joy does not finally depend upon what we do with our freedom. In fact, Old Testament writers picture God laughing at the foolish who hate His knowledge (Prov. 1:24-26), at the rulers who rebel against His chosen leader (Ps. 2:1-4), and at the wicked who plot against the righteous (37:12-13).

These images of what seems to be derisive laughter may trouble you. How could a God of love laugh at those who are rejecting His love? It is a disturbing thought. What we must recognize is that the biblical writers had a very difficult task "portraying" God. They had only human language and known human experience to use in describing what God is like and what He does. Both the language and the experience are inadequate, which is one reason why the Scriptures can be understood only through the interpretation of the Holy Spirit. God's laughter at those who sin against Him really exposes a profound sadness, as when we say, "If I didn't laugh, I'd cry." Laughter and tears are often very close to one another. If God laughs over the presumption of our sin, He is weeping underneath.

LAUGHING PROVIDENCE

Actually the laughter of God, grounded as it is in reality and acquainted with pain, is a great source of comfort to us. Because God can laugh at great obstacles and strong enemies, we can feel secure. When faced with those who would destroy him, the psalmist David turns to God and says, "You laugh at them, O LORD; you hold all the nations in derision. O my strength, I will watch for you; for you, O God, are my fortress" (59:8-9).

The laughter of God tells us all that things are under control; it's the sign of His providence.

It is also His gift to us. The psalmist wrote, "Our mouth was filled with laughter" (126:2). He gives us suitable times for laughing (Eccles. 3:4). He promises us that after weeping we will be blessed with laughter (Luke 6:21). He even makes it possible for us to laugh at the powerful who trust in abundant riches and seek refuge in wealth (Ps. 52:6-7).

We can laugh God's laugh. We can be so awestruck by the humanly improbable promises He makes that we roll over in laughter. How else can we be expected to act? When God appeared to Abraham and told him that his wife, Sarah, would bear a son and that by doing so she would give rise to nations, he "fell on his face and laughed." Why? Because he was 99 years of age, and Sarah was 90! (Gen. 17:15-17).

It gets even better when three mysterious messengers visit Abraham and Sarah's encampment by the oaks of Mamre (18:1-15). There's no indication Abraham knew who they were, but he treats them with that extreme courtesy and hospitality for which the East is known: a good footwashing followed by a table spread with bread, cakes, veal, curds, and milk. They ask about his wife, Sarah, who, by the way, has been back in the tent slaving over this sumptuous meal without even a spare moment to come and say hello. They are curious about her absence, and Abraham tells them where she is. I personally think this assured them that she was close enough to eavesdrop, because one of them drops that bomb out of the blue again, the one about the baby. Obviously Abraham has not shared the earlier visitation and message with Sarah, because when she hears the promise from this visitor, she's completely thrown for a loop. She laughs. Hardly able to contain herself, she says, "After I have grown old, and my husband is old, shall I have pleasure?" (v. 12).

The visitors have very good hearing themselves. One whom the Bible identifies as "the LORD" asks Abraham, "Why did Sarah laugh, and say, 'Shall I indeed bear a child, now that I am old?'" (v. 13). He follows this with a reminder that the subject here is Almighty God, and he says it loudly enough for Sarah to hear: "Is anything too wonderful for the LORD? At the set time I will return to you, in due season, and Sarah shall have a son" (v. 14).

Now Sarah is embarrassed by her laughter and is afraid she has insulted their guests. She tries to pretend that it was not really laughter they had heard. How could they distinguish what was happening on the other side of the tent wall? "I did not laugh," she protests (v. 15).

But it's a feeble disclaimer; her laughter is not to be denied. It's God's gift. It's the sign of His improbable providence. "Oh yes, you did laugh," says the visitor (v. 15). I imagine he knew what lay beneath that laugh—the decades of unfulfilled hope, the shame of a promise that never was delivered, the hurt, the faith reduced to a very thin thread. As it sometimes is with us, the laughter is an eruption of hope that Sarah hardly dares to believe in. It is both an uncontrollable expression of the hope and a protection against being denied it once again. If she laughs, no one will know how completely wedded she is to the hope; no one will see her heart break again. Her laugh lets the cat out of the bag safely. Dare she hope again?

The child is born next spring.

The laughter of Abraham and Sarah has echoed down the centuries, the laughter of God given to those He loves who dare to believe, the laughter that is a gift to us as well: "Now Sarah said, 'God has brought laughter for me; everyone who hears will laugh with me'" (21:6).

You and I are invited to laugh the laughter of God. Before our very eyes He does something impossible, creates the incredible, snatches victory from the jaws of defeat—and invites us to join Him in a good laugh. The temptation of our disbelieving nature is to refuse to accept the grounds for laughter, to deny providence, even when it stares us in the face. With cynical hearts we say, "Don't make me laugh." We turn and walk away from the gift.

LAUGHING MESSIAH

The New Testament has something to say about that. It says that God decided to do something about our willful sadness, that the second Person of the Trinity entered human life as one of us. And one of the things He brought was laughter.

I must confess that it was a long time before I could see humor in the life and ministry of Jesus. He was the Son of God on serious business. He was perfect, for heaven's sake! He was just so—well, *divine!* And He was following a divinely ordained plan for redeeming the world. There was no time for foolishness or fun. Or so I thought.

As I've grown older, I have allowed Jesus to become more human in my own thinking. Strangely, at the same time His divinity has become even more convincing to me. Perhaps to say it more accurately, I have allowed *myself* greater freedom to experience His humanity, to understand Him as a historical Person, to interact with His story, to come to terms with the similarities be-tween His life and mine.

It seems to me that as the Church became farther and far-ther removed from the time of Jesus' earthly life, its view of Jesus became more sacral and stylized. It is not at all surprising that the hottest theological debate during the early centuries of the Church had to do with the identity and definition of the person of Jesus. The greatest tendency was to make Him appear as holy and removed as possible and to stylize Him—to create a consis-tent image of Him so as to avoid or correct misinterpretation. It was necessary to take steps of this kind in order to be as clear as possible about who the God-Man was and in order to combat heresy about Him. But the fallout was to make Him less real on a human level, to depict Him as removed from us—and, of course, to eliminate almost all humor from His person. Walk through the cathedrals of Europe and try to find any joy or delight in the thousands upon thousands of paintings and sculptures of Jesus. You will be hard-pressed to do so.

James H. Rutz makes an interesting observation about Christian art in the early centuries after Christ. He says that you see an evolution in how artists depicted our Lord at supper. In the earliest depictions, Jesus is having a good time. But as time goes on, more and more you see "a dismal Christ in the upper room staring morbidly at a cup, with the dozen around him sober-faced and sad."[1]

I'm convinced that the earliest representations were closer to the truth. Jesus had a sense of humor. You can see it in some of His teachings. As His example of where *not* to pray, He de-scribes a self-conscious Pharisee picking the prayer locations where the less pious are most likely to observe and admire his piety: in the synagogue and on a busy street corner. I can't imag-ine His hearers not chuckling over that characterization (with the exception of a few Pharisees who may have been listening at a distance!) and being helped by the humor to get the point of prayer as a genuine, not self-conscious, communion with the Heavenly Father. Then He pokes good-natured fun at the Gen-tiles who "heap up empty phrases . . . for they think that they will be heard because of their many words" (Matt. 6:7).

"Now think about it," says Jesus as He chuckles. "We're

dealing with *God* here! Don't you think your Father knows what you need before you ask Him? So why would you presume to increase His understanding, to help Him see things better than He already does? Are you going to educate God?" By now Jesus probably has the crowd laughing—and learning.

Jesus was also capable of a certain playfulness in His interaction with people. Take for instance His encounters with children. He loved the people to bring children to Him, and when they did, He often honored them by saying, "Of such is the kingdom of heaven," or by using their simple, trusting faith as a model for adults to follow. I would be surprised if on these occasions He didn't have some playful interaction with the children of whom He spoke. He had them brought forward not merely as object lessons but as persons to talk with. I believe He enjoyed them and shared some playful moments with them. I'm sure He gave some wise advice in language they could understand—but He also entered their special world of play. But this was the best thing He did: "He took them up in his arms, laid his hands on them, and blessed them" (Mark 10:16). He may have even bounced them on His knee and told them a funny parable.

We see the laughter of God throughout the ministry of Jesus. God laughs when four men get their paralyzed friend to Jesus by literally breaking through the roof (Mark 2:3-12). He laughs when Jesus eats with tax collectors and sinners, the lowest of the low, and the Pharisees are left scratching their heads—they just don't get it! (vv. 15-17). He laughs when the disciples of John imply that Jesus' disciples are not quite up to par because they don't fast often—and Jesus talks about new patches sewn on old cloth making an even worse tear (vv. 18, 21). I think I hear Him laugh when I take myself too seriously, and something happens to lighten me up and loosen my grip. He laughs again and again, because life with Him is ever new, always surprising, never dull, often hilarious.

But there's one thing that brings God the greatest joy: He laughs with pure delight when He sees Jesus liberating one more soul from sin's sadness. In fact, He calls the hosts of heaven to a party—and the universe echoes with His laughter (Luke 15:7).

3

The God Who Can Play a Joke

D o you find the idea of God playing a joke to be irreverent, even disrespectful? A jokester, you could say, is the last person you would want to identify God with. God would not make fun at someone else's expense.

True enough. God isn't like that. But I hope this chapter will help to convince you that He knows how to joke. He sees the humor in life situations. He has a funny side that comes out again and again. So do we (remember: we're made in His image!), and if we're going to *be* like Him and *act* like Him, we're going to have to learn how to have fun, see the humor in life, and laugh at good jokes.

A Life of Surprises

Good jokes are worth telling. Funny stories are worth repeating. Life is forever turning out differently than we expect, and jokes are one way we have of honoring that fact. A good joke celebrates life's surprises, and the punch line throws us off balance by redefining the real center. Just when we think we have a situation figured out, wham!—the punch line, the unexpected, the outcome we had not planned on, the reminder that life is so much more than calculated outcomes. We all need a good joke every now and then.

Jokes turn on the element of genuine surprise. So does life. The surprise in a joke's punch line plays either on an unexpected outcome or on a human foible. Sometimes the unexpected outcome is a moment of serendipity. Usually the exposed foible helps us to laugh at ourselves, to admit the ridiculousness of our pretense and presumption. All this is worth experiencing because it's the truth and we need to know it. Though life has its moments of tragedy and pain, it is also a caravan of serendipity, a string of strange surprises that keep us laughing. Mostly, we need to laugh at the puzzles of our own humanity, our own unpredictability, our contradictions, the humor of our always failing schemes and of our always flawed self-manufactured righteousness. They all deserve a good laugh.

HEALTH THROUGH HUMOR

It's also worth remembering that humor is good for our health. I remember reading about the amazing experience of Norman Cousins. The well-known author and diplomat suddenly became ill following a particularly strenuous assignment in Russia. The doctor's diagnosis was shattering: a collagen disease that was virtually terminal; only 1 in 500 persons with the disease recovered. Cousins decided he would not give in—he would fight this dread enemy. He did three things. The first was to think positive thoughts, the second was to take massive doses of vitamin C—and the third was *to laugh!* Lying flat on his back with the persistent pain of aching spine and joints, he watched hour after hour of *Candid Camera* replays and slapstick comedies like the old Laurel and Hardy films. And he read book after book of jokes. The result was a miraculous recovery. Since that time, I understand, the therapeutic value of humor has been the subject of scientific study, and the hypothesis has been substantiated: humor heals. As the writer of Proverbs noted, "A cheerful heart is a good medicine" (17:22).

It makes sense to me that the One who is the source of all healing has a robust sense of humor. It also makes sense that where this Healer has been turned from and abandoned, there would be precious little real humor. The verse in Proverbs just quoted ends "but a downcast spirit dries up the bones."

THE HUMORLESSNESS OF SIN

The trouble with sinners is that they can't take a joke. "Sour godliness," said John Wesley, "is the devil's religion." Why is this so? I think George MacDonald knew the answer when he wrote, "It is the heart that is unsure of his God that is afraid to laugh"[1]—afraid to laugh, perhaps, because there is little to laugh about. When the laughing God seems far away, life becomes too serious with the weight of our self-reliance. We hear only occasional faint echoes of His laughter. Life without God is depressingly somber.

You might wonder about that and say, "It seems to me that a lot of sinners are having a great deal of fun!" So it seems at first. My own conviction is that where genuine humor emerges in a fallen world, it's an intimation of Kingdom joy, an enticing sample of grace, a touch of gospel inviting the world to come home to God's fun-loving family. It's God calling us back to joy.[2] But there is also a "dark" humor in the world, a humor that feasts on our degradation, verbally exploits the weak, brutally stereotypes and scorns those who are different (as, for example, in racist jokes), and stupidly portrays the gutter of the mind as the playground of real fun. This is the shadowy side of genuine laughter. It is what humor becomes without God, an attempt to have fun by inventing a false reason. It is really no fun at all.[3]

The good news of the gospel is that the real fun is back. Why else do you think Luke tells us about a multitude of the heavenly host announcing Jesus' birth with a choral symphony of praise? "Glory to God in the highest heaven, and on earth peace among those whom he favors!" (2:14). Why else do we see shepherds, magi, a priest, an elderly prophet, and who knows who else on the scene, dancing the rhythm and singing the melody of jubilation over promise fulfillment? The joy is back!

Now I would not try to diminish the difficulty this birth caused Joseph and Mary: the personal embarrassment of an early pregnancy; the arduous journey from Nazareth to Bethlehem just before delivery; the further embarrassment and discomfort of delivery in a crude, smelly stable; the sudden flight to Egypt due to the fact that even at this early time in their child's life, the ruling monarch sensed a rival threat and ordered wholesale murder. No, the Incarnation, the enfleshment of God, was not an easy event for Mary and Joseph, and they will always be honored for obeying God and cradling His Son at great personal cost. But they did it with willing hearts because they had each been visited by a messenger from God with incredibly good news that the Child in Mary's womb was the hope of Israel who would "save his people from their sins" (Matt. 1:21). Mary was so overwhelmed with joy that she sang a beautiful song that began, "My soul magnifies the Lord, and my spirit rejoices in God my Savior" (Luke 1:46-47). Jesus' parents put up with a lot because they had a lot to look forward to. And when the Child was born, their hearts danced for joy.

In fact, the entire universe probably danced—or at least those who sensed what was really going on in Bethlehem did. There is a wonderful painting of the event by Sandro Botticelli called *Mystic Nativity*, displayed in the National Art Gallery in London. The painting takes in not only the stable but also the surroundings. Given the relatively small size of the work, the detail is brilliant. The focal point, of course, is the Child in the stall, but what makes the scene so unusual is what is going on outside the humble shed. Everywhere angels are dancing in groups—in the skies, on the roof of the stable, around the stable, and in the foreground. Also in the foreground are little demonic figures scampering for the futile protection of crevices and caves. Botticelli's canvas and oils reveal lavish universal joy.

In the same gallery is a Nativity scene by Piero della Francesca. If Botticelli's Nativity scene captures the universe singing, Francesca's captures the humor. His work is a close-up of the stable itself. All the characters are there; the scene is glorious. But if you look closely behind the Madonna, the shepherds, and the ox, you will see a donkey peeking out from behind the shoulder of an angel. Its head is thrown back, its mouth is wide open, and its teeth are gleaming. It's obviously braying as loudly and as gloriously as it can.

Now why didn't Francesca do the usual thing and have all the animals simply standing by or staring in silent wonder at the manger? Why is this donkey, one of the most laughable of beasts, the object of countless jokes, making such a shocking gesture of hilarity? How could the painter make the Incarnation such a joking matter? Doesn't he grasp what this is all about?

I think he *does* grasp what this Nativity event is all about. I think he sees behind it a God who knows how to play a joke. The "joke" is simply this: here in this least suspected place, by the least suspected means, to the least suspected couple, in the least suspected company—enters the Messiah of God, the Savior of the world! If a donkey can get it, why can't we? No wonder Botticelli's little demons were fooled and totally caught off guard: the punch line was the beginning of their end. Three cheers for the donkey who saw it—and understood! As Frederick Buechner says, "Blessed is he who gets the joke."[4]

JESUS' HUMOR

The humor of God, unleashed in the Nativity, is seen again and again in the adult life of Jesus. Most of the Messiah's humor was verbal, but sometimes His punch lines were visual—as, for example, when He turned water into wine. Not everyone saw Him do it, and the steward was simply amazed that somehow the bridegroom had found such superior wine to serve toward the end. Mum's the word, but Jesus' disciples saw Him do it (this was His first miracle), and the Gospel writer comments that it "revealed his glory; and his disciples believed in him" (John 2:11).

Jesus was the great puller of surprises. His disciples were never quite sure what He was going to do next. Following Jesus is a training in the unexpected. There is the tumult and near arrest caused by the Master's fiery condemnation of the religious establishment. The next thing you know, He tenderly addresses a group of children and tells His disciples that these little ones are the stuff of the Kingdom. Then we're at a scene in which Jesus exorcises the long-resident demon of a completely deranged and dangerous man, at which time a herd of swine become possessed of these same demons and go charging over the cliff. Next thing you know He's sitting on the side of some mountain and shocking everyone with unheard-of, radical lifestyle teaching.

And so it goes, all the way to the last hours of His life, to His final meal with His beloved disciples, when He removes His outer robe, ties a towel around himself, pours water into a basin, and washes their feet. *No, Lord—You must not do this! It's the servant's job!* And a few hours later, the final shocker: cruel death on a cross. *Lord, why have You let this sinful world disgrace You so? And why have You left us alone?* But finally, a few days later, another shocker: a living Lord, Jesus resurrected! *But we thought You were gone! Was it not a dead body we placed in the tomb?*

Jesus—the greatest puller of surprises the world has ever seen.

FUNNY STORIES

Jesus also knew how to tell a funny story. He didn't do it just to get people laughing. He was not some kind of messianic stand-up comedian. His use of such hilarious images as a camel going through the eye of a needle had a point. (No pun intended!) People obsessed with their wealth would find the kingdom of God just as difficult to enter.

Jesus loved to tell stories about suppers and banquets. Once He told one about a man who decides to have a sumptuous feast and invite all his friends[5] (Luke 14:16-24). The dinner invitations are sent out, and the feast day arrives. A very large sum of money has been expended on food and decorations, not to mention entertainment. The host sends his trusty slaves to announce to his invited friends, "Come; for everything is ready now" (v. 17). The feast of the year has arrived! The host's doorman prepares for a stampede.

No stampede. Every one of the invited guests, it seems, has "better" things to do. One says to the messenger, "I have bought a piece of land, and I must go out and see it; please accept my regrets." (Jesus' audience is probably thinking, "He would rather go look at a piece of land, which will still be there tomorrow, than to be at this once-in-a-lifetime mother of all feasts? How foolish!") Another says to the messenger, "I have bought five yoke of oxen, and I am going to try them out; please accept my regrets." (Same incredulity from the audience, who by now are probably snickering and snorting.) The response from a third invitee may threaten to break up the whole teaching session, because this response baits all the amateur comedians in the crowd: "I have just been married, and therefore I cannot come." ("Cannot come? *Cannot come?*" shouts one comedian from the crowd. "It didn't take her long to put you under lock and key, did it?" Another pipes in, "Take her with you, stupid—or is she too homely to be seen with?" Now the crowd's in stitches. How in the world is Jesus going to bring them back around?)

"Guess what the host does!" shouts Jesus over the uproarious commotion He has created with His humor. The crowd eventually quiets down. They're all ears. "He sends his servants into the streets and lanes, especially the worst ones in town, and tells them to 'bring in the poor, the crippled, the blind, and the lame' [v. 21]. That's exactly what the servants do; and still there's room. 'Go out into the roads and lanes,' the host says, 'and compel people to come in, so that my house may be filled. For I tell you, none of those who were invited will taste my dinner'" (vv. 23-24).

As I picture the setting of this storytelling session in my mind, I see the crowd stunned into wondering silence. The punch line is sinking in. A laugh is heard. Then another. In no time flat just about everyone is joining in, including Jesus. Laughter is everywhere. It's a very different kind of laughter, the laughter of the gospel, the laughter of the poor, the crippled, the blind, the lame, the forgotten—the laughter of earth's excluded—who suddenly realize they are the *most* included! It is the laughter that rings through God's universe and resonates with the laughter of heaven. And all of us self-righteous bigots who have been standing around the edges of that crowd wondering how we could possibly civilize, "respectify," accommodate, tame, dilute, and legalize Jesus' teaching, and not allow it to undermine our hard-earned standing, are suddenly shocked by a realization. We now know that we come to God on the same basis as do those we have considered at best the unfortunates of the world and at worst the dregs of society. The tables of our smug exclusiveness are completely turned!

Jesus certainly did know how to tell a joke. Like Father, like Son. And the punch lines live on as gospel.

Messianic Misfit

The life of Jesus is permeated with scenes that have twinges of humor. Let's look at another. Once again, Jesus is at a table with publicans[6] and sinners (Matt. 9:10-13; Luke 15:1-2). What's funny about the scene is that Jesus always seems to be having a very good time, so much so that the scribes and Pharisees are dumbfounded. How could this so-called Messiah find pleasure in such company? How could a restorer of righteousness associate so freely with lowlife?

The funny thing is—He's right at home. Mind you, He does occasionally take a meal in the home of a Pharisee, but it seems that something always goes wrong, that there's always some way Jesus doesn't fit in to the appropriate social convention and etiquette of this polite and pure society (Luke 7:36-50; 11:37-54; 14:1-24). Don't you think the people notice where Jesus is most accepted and appreciated and where He's not? And don't you think it brings a smile to their faces? Especially when the scribes and Pharisees get really overwrought about those dinners with the "rabble," and spew the venom of their self-righteousness: "Look, a glutton and a drunkard, a friend of tax collectors and sinners!" (Matt. 11:19; Luke 7:34). They just can't grasp that the Kingdom Jesus is preaching and living is open and that this is the *only* way He'll have it.

Come on, scribes and Pharisees! Break free from your old dogmas. Better still, hear the flute and dance. Jesus is playing the Kingdom tune for you; He wants you to dance (Matt. 11:17; Luke 7:32). In fact, He wants to dance *with* you.

Caller to the Dance

Sydney Carter hears Jesus call the dance and puts the call into these words:

"I danced in the morning when the world was begun,
And I danced in the moon and the stars and the sun,
And I came down from Heaven and I danced on the earth.
At Bethlehem I had my birth.

"Dance, then, wherever you may be;
I am the Lord of the Dance," said He,
"And I'll lead you all wherever you may be,
And I'll lead you all in the Dance," said He.

"I danced for the scribe and the Pharisee,
But they would not dance and they would not follow me,
I danced for the fishermen, for James and John;
They came to me and the Dance went on." *

*© 1963 Stainer and Bell, Ltd. Admin. by Hope Publishing Co., Carol Stream, IL 60188. All rights reserved. Used by permission.

And so it was: from the dawn of creation, to Bethlehem, through the hills and valleys and plains of Palestine, even to that final hill of death, He danced. He danced around scribes and Pharisees and invited them to join Him, but their feet were too glued to the ground of their own false goodness. He danced for some humble fishermen, and they dropped their nets and followed. It took them awhile to learn the steps, and sometimes they got their feet terribly crossed up, but they kept their eyes on the Dance Instructor and finally learned. He danced for everyone, and to those who put aside their cautions and fears, He gave power to become the frolickers and flingers of His kingdom.

He has always danced. And He dances for us today. He is the Son of the dancing God, the God who knows how to have a good time, even how to play a good joke. He is the God who wants us to enjoy it all—the dances He calls and the jokes He plays.

Part 2

Hilarity
on Earth

4

First Innocence

faith has as much to say about our earthly beginnings as does science. Science pursues the measurement of the observable; faith grapples with the life of the soul. The science of acoustics, for example, is concerned with analyzing the sound waves and their combinations in a Beethoven symphony, but Beethoven invites us to share the vision he is constructing with his artistry of vibrations. The chemistry of color reveals the complex mixes of ingredients that create a magnificent Turner sunset, but Turner beckons us to a far greater revelation, one that grips our soul. The story is told of a lady visiting an exhibit of Turner's paintings. The artist was standing near her when she remarked, "I never saw such colors in a sunset."

He replied, "Madam, don't you wish you *could?*"

What you see is what you get. It's not that you see what you want to see; it's that you see what you allow yourself to see—there's always far more than meets the eye. The Bible invites us to allow ourselves to see reality through the eyes of faith. It is not that science sees things objectively and faith subjectively. Science itself is in a state of unending flux and clashes of theories. Today's scientific "truths" become tomorrow's outmoded speculations. Some scientists have come to believe that the universe is far more clever than we are and that we will never figure it out; and many of them believe that the nature of the universe is inseparable from our consciousness of it. Physicist Charles Townes concluded, "I do not understand how the scientific approach alone, as separated from a religious approach, can explain an origin of all things."[1]

What does Christian faith say about our beginnings? It points us to the beginning of the Bible, where we follow God on a whirlwind of Creation-making, with no hints of how He did it—leaving future scientists to their field days of speculation—and brings us to the crowning achievement when God says, "Let us make humankind in our image, according to our likeness; and let them have dominion" (Gen. 1:26). It leads us to a garden where a story is told, a story of imparted glory and innocence. This is the beginning that defines us.

INNOCENCE

You might think that a claim of first innocence is founded on pure fiction and dreamy visions of humanity's primal purity. Has our view of the human race sunk so low that we've come to expect that everyone is driven by the most elementary and the basest self-centered instincts, always and inevitably falling short of the glory of God? Have our outlooks become so jaundiced and our actions so duplicitous that we retain no inkling of a singular innocence, a purity of thought? Does the idea of a holy innocence only bring a smirk on our faces because we reckon that the human race is so contaminated with compromise that innocence has not got a lick of a chance and that any claim to it is obviously self-serving hypocrisy?

Or do we have our moments when innocence does break in like a shaft of pure, unspoiled light? Do we sometimes see intimations of glory and primal dignity? Does an incredibly unselfish act of human kindness or unselfconscious self-sacrifice stir within us a vision of a nobility for which we may have been intended? Or does the moment of observing a child's unrepressed delight when the child's parents commit an act of loving affirmation put you in touch with the innocence that years of cautious, self-protective restraint have kept buried deep within you?

The story in the garden begins with the glory and the innocence of our race. The characters, Adam and Eve, are children of innocence. They know only the good, because they allow themselves to know only God. They're endowed with glory because they're free and use that freedom to glorify God by living in obedience to Him. And they love each other with a pure human love, untarnished by duplicity—"And the man and his wife were both naked, and were not ashamed" (Gen. 2:25). They know the deepest joy of their relationship with God, as well as their relationship with one another. Adam can hardly hide his delight when Eve enters his world: "This at last" (v. 23). In the beginning were glory and innocence—and joy.

MYSTERY

There was also mystery. Adam's exclamation spoke more than pure joy; it spoke deep wonder. This Creator-God who lovingly fashions us and calls us into existence is at the same time a mystery whom we can spend an eternity getting to know; and this human "other" in our lives, this Eve or this Adam, this one to whom we are powerfully drawn and with whom we can become most intimately acquainted, will forever be, like God, a mystery. To presume to have figured anyone out is presumption of the highest order, an illusion that always backfires.

In the beginning was the wonder, the mystery, the miracle of each other. What we really know and can enjoy is that each of us is some kind of wonder whom the One who created us alone fully knows; and every one of us, with the same just cause, can sing with the psalmist, "You . . . formed my inward parts; you knit me together in my mother's womb. I praise you, for I am fearfully and wonderfully made. Wonderful are your works; that I know very well. My frame was not hidden from you, when I was being made in secret, intricately woven in the depths of the earth" (139:13-15).

We need not fear our unknown, which God knows. We are His domain, His delight, there for endless discovery. This is our glory, and to embrace it is to feel the touch of innocent wonder once again.

WORLD OF WONDER

But don't stop there. The whole world is swimming in wonder! Come at it through any one of your senses, and you have a nonstop procession of new stimuli that keep your nervous system working and your brain interested: sound waves in an infinite variety of rhythms, pitches, timbres, combinations, and progressions; light waves that flood the eyes with rapid successions of framed form, color, and shade in endless transition; touches that bring an abundant array of textures to our fingertips; tastes that reveal the rich essence of creation's vast cuisine; smells that unlock its permeating aromas. But those senses of ours are in a kind of captivity to our will and to the confining expectations of our minds. We mostly hear, see, touch, taste, and smell what we allow ourselves to, and we're highly selective. So the life of our senses, if too carefully filtered, becomes almost predictable, dull. And we lose touch with this swimming-in-wonder world. We don't give our senses much scope.

Annie Dillard writes of the unfathomable profligacy and intricacy of nature. As she journeys in nature around her place in the Virginia Appalachians and reads the naturalists and biologists, she braves the disarming of her comprehension: the more she allows herself to see and understand, the more she realizes that she doesn't understand.

> The creator goes off on one wild, specific tangent after another, or millions simultaneously, with an exuberance that would seem to be unwarranted, and with an abandoned energy sprung from an unfathomable font. What is going on here? The point of the dragonfly's terrible lip, the giant water bug, birdsong, or the beautiful dazzle and flash of sunlighted minnows, is not that it all fits together like clockwork . . . but that it all flows so freely wild, like the creek, that it all surges in such a free, fringed tangle. Freedom is the world's water and weather, the world's nourishment freely given, its soil and sap: and the creator loves pizzazz.[2]

If only God were fixed, if only He were simply "the Unmoved Mover" of the universe, we could over time figure Him out. But He is not, and we are left with multiple mysteries—and faith, if we dare to have it.

In a universe of mysterious extravagance, faith is not a desperate search for the fixed, a grasping at something that can be nailed down and put to rest, like a body in a coffin. It is a reckless embrace of the free, a hanging on for dear life while God dances and shows us one improbable step after another. Faith is nothing less than dancing with trusting abandon on the dance floor of God's universe.

ECSTASY

There is also ecstasy here. We find it in the Bible too: prophets in a frenzy (1 Sam. 10:5-13), David leaping and dancing before the Lord (2 Sam. 6:12-16), Ezekiel's trances (Ezek. 2:2; 3:14, 23-27), Jeremiah drunk with the Word of God (Jer. 23:9), Zechariah speechless for days over the enormity of what he has seen and heard (Luke 1:5-20), Jesus' baptismal trance (Mark 1:9-11), Peter's vision of all creation's sanctity (Acts 10:11-16), Paul's life-transforming vision (Acts 9:1-9) and his transportation to heaven (2 Cor. 12:1-4).[3] What is this all about?

Each ecstasy is different, carrying its own revelation. But maybe they're also the same. Maybe they all penetrate the patinas and pretenses of our daily concourse and bring the person to a place of holy innocence in which nothing obstructs the beginning where pure joy reigns, and for those moments sin does not tarnish the image of who we are and what we're about. It is as if, briefly, we are unfallen.

Dangerous stuff, these ecstasies. One can come out of them above the ground and putting on airs. There's the danger of relentlessly pursuing the euphoria and fabricating the experience. We cannot finally *make* our joy—it's a gift of God. Authentic ecstasy is God's given moment.

Here's the catch: He gives joy to the obedient. Joy without obedience is fiction. Euphoric Christians who are not living seriously as disciples of Jesus are at best deluded and at worst pretending. Prophets and apostles had to put their lives on the line and risk the consequences of their brave ecstasies and boundary-breaking visions. Joy without obedience is a desperate substitute of the cheap and quick for the costly and enduring.

Perhaps obedience is the hardest part of joy. Adam and Eve were placed in the garden of ecstasy, but there was forbidden fruit (Gen. 2:15-17). Ecstasy has limits. Joy at the beginning is not a private indulgence; it's an enjoyment of God and His creation, a celebration of our being His creatures and a disavowal of any pretension to divinity. Only at such a place can there be joy. The serpent knows what he's doing, then, when offering the forbidden fruit and falsely promising immortality: "You will not die" (3:4).

DELUSION AND DUPLICITY

The serpent also promises that Adam's and Eve's eyes will be opened and that they "will be like God, knowing good and evil" (3:5). He's right—and he's wrong. Yes, they will indeed become worldly-wise, always seeing and being tempted by the possible disobedience in every call to obedience. But no, they will not see with the clarity and delight of the innocent, with the creature-vision without which there can be no real joy. Their vision, their knowledge, their motives, their actions—the whole complex bundle—are now compromised. Innocence is lost, duplicity found. To everything there is now an angle. Every conversation has a hidden agenda. Every motive is mixed. Every action is cautious and calculated.

The irony of our Fall is that, "knowing good and evil," we don't really know anything! We grope in the dark knowing neither where we are nor where we're going. Or to use Emil Brunner's metaphor, we are "dogs in a great art gallery," surrounded by a world of revelation but able to see only the means the Painter used, not the vision toward which He is pointing us.[4] The apostle Paul says we became senseless in our thinking and that our minds were darkened. Claiming to be wise, we became fools and exchanged the glory of the immortal God for our own images of reality (Rom. 1:21-23).

It's a scene of utter delusion, leading inevitably and relentlessly to despair. Shattered hopes leave us with nothing to grasp and everything to grieve over. The utterly strange claim of Scripture is that when obedience goes, so does joy. A fallen race pursues its own course, each one of us defining his or her own allegiance and forcing his or her own idea of a destiny, all the while imagining that this is the freedom that makes the heart glad.

RETURN TO THE BEGINNING

But our hearts know differently: joy comes when we discover the freedom of knowing we are not God and when, relieved of this burden, we liberate ourselves to enjoy living in His presence and responding to His unusual claims. To put it simply, joy comes with holiness of life, which is utter responsiveness to God. This indeed is true joy, and whenever we manage to touch it, we touch what life is meant to be. We touch the beginning.

5

The Pursuit of Happiness

For most, joy seems a faded memory. The pleasurable Edens seem far away and rarely accessible. But now and then, in spite of impaired vision, a glimpse is caught of the glory lost, and in spite of heavy hearts, a lift is given by the unanticipated intrusion of joy. But these are rare moments. Joy is largely forgotten.

You can see a poignant description of why this is when you read in Gen. 3:16-19 the account of the curse under which the human race now lives following the Fall in Eden. It is difficult to imagine how such drudgery and pain leaves any room for joy. Joy is a luxury we do not deserve, cannot afford, and rarely know. Despair is sin's rightful bequest to us.

THE CULTURE OF HAPPINESS

How do we live in this state? How do we survive without joy? Fallen humanity has invented ways. One is to pursue happiness. When joy is lost, happiness becomes a preoccupation, often an obsession, our desperate attempt to replace the hilarity of our lost innocence. The attempt does not succeed—it never does—but we are in no condition to admit it. Given our circumstances, we take what we can get.

It comes as no surprise that there is a culture of happiness in the Western world. Dedicated to the pursuit of personal well-being, this culture makes the pursuit of happiness a relentless obsession. This infatuation with one's blessings is not unknown in Scripture. The Jew of the Old Testament tended to equate social and physical prosperity with God's approval and favor. (See, for example, Gen. 24:35.) The recognition that often the wicked prosper and the righteous do not creates a crisis for all forms of "prosperity theology." The even more difficult fact that the righteous are sometimes dealt terrible misfortune calls into serious question the proposition that our condition of life has anything to do with how well we have lived before God. The terrible ordeals of righteous Job disarm prosperity thinking and point the way to the Messiah who emptied himself of all prosperity and took upon himself the form of a slave (Phil. 2:7). The only prosperity the Scriptures finally embrace for this life's journey is that of the heart. The apostle Paul reviews all his ancestral, educational, social, and positional advantages—all forms of prosperity that were his—and simply says that for the sake of the only prosperity that matters, the prosperity of "knowing Christ Jesus my Lord," the other is "rubbish" (3:4-8).

THE SEARCH FOR SATISFACTION

This kind of thinking, of course, goes against the grain of the prevailing search for blessings. People worry not only about their economic survival but also about having sufficient wealth to indulge themselves and signal their success. Wealth, in other words, is the key to happiness. I read recently about a survey conducted by an organization in Hong Kong on attitudes to happiness throughout Asia. The study found that an astonishing 94 percent of those surveyed in Indonesia, one of the poorest countries, said they were happy. The unhappiest were those surveyed in Japan, the richest country in the region. Richard Adeney, who cites the study, says, "It makes you wonder if there is an inverse correlation between wealth and happiness."[1]

The culture of happiness drives more than the search for wealth. Many people marry in order to find happiness. They hope the marriage partner they have found will be the one who will bring them blessing and satisfaction. They enter marriage with high expectations for the rewards they expect it to bring. All too often—the data say about 50 percent of the time in the Western world—the marriage fails and ends in divorce. Of those who stay together for life, some never come close to the bliss that was hoped for at the beginning. The institution of marriage has no ability of itself to bring us joy.

Surely religion is the answer. Surely it is the true source of joy. As William James pointed out years ago, many people "come to regard the happiness which a religious belief affords as a proof of its truth. If a creed makes a man feel happy, he almost inevitably adopts it."[2] But alas, when we embrace Christianity to find happiness, it disappoints us. Christian faith is not an allegiance entered into for our own selfish (even though harmless) ends. It's the giving of ourselves to God and His ends. We violate the Christian religion when we embrace it in any other way and for any other purpose. It is not a means to our ends.[3]

But one need not confine himself or herself to the Christian religion in the quest for happiness. There's an almost unlimited smorgasbord of New Age religions and prosperity theologies to pick from—all of them promising complete happiness vis-à-vis their fulfillment formulas.

ADDICTION TO HAPPINESS

The alcoholic sobers to pain, the food addict lives with the discomfort and bodily damage caused by excess, the power seeker lives with the emptiness of the never-sufficient influence acquired, the person driven by sexual obsession is never satisfied by self-indulgence, and the codependent, the person addicted to relationships, never finds a relationship that brings real joy. All addictions are an escape from painful issues, a desperate pursuit of painlessness, and they always fail to deliver.

So it is with the addiction to happiness. The obsessive pursuit of it is a desperate affair. We try to stay as many steps ahead of disaster as possible. We work overtime to outrun financial ruin, buy insurance policies to head off disastrous losses, eat healthful foods and get regular medical checkups to ward off catastrophic illnesses, go to church just in case there is a God who has a hand in our fortunes, or even attend retreats or self-help seminars to help us keep our lives together and nurture a positive environment for ourselves. It's not enough to expect happiness—we must also work for it; we must do the right things to ensure it. But no matter how diligently and doggedly we pursue it, like a dog chasing its tail, it eludes us. Just when we think we have achieved happiness, misfortune appears from nowhere and snatches it away. Happiness seems to bring with it, and inevitably succumbs to, its own opposite. No wonder Solomon observed that "even in laughter the heart is sad" (Prov. 14:13). Jesus aimed some words at those who thought they had found happiness: "Woe to you who are laughing now, for you will mourn and weep" (Luke 6:25). Happiness does not last.

Ecclesiastes sees the culture of happiness as idolatry and the pursuit of happiness as vanity. In the second chapter of that book of reality checks, the writer says to himself, "Come now, I will make a test of pleasure; enjoy yourself" (Eccles. 2:1). He pursues happiness in all its forms: "Whatever my eyes desired I did not keep from them; I kept my heart from no pleasure, for my heart found pleasure in all my toil, and this was my reward for all my toil" (v. 10). Finally, he comes to his sobering conclusion: "Then I considered all that my hands had done and the toil I had spent in doing it, and again, all was vanity and a chasing after wind, and there was nothing to be gained under the sun" (v. 11). The search for happiness ends in futility.

The Culture of Avoidance

How is it, then, that the culture of happiness not only survives but is prosperous? If it inevitably fails, how is the myth kept alive? The answer is that we assiduously cultivate the capacity to avoid reality—we learn to "fake it."

The culture of avoidance has been with us since the Fall. It does not take each of us long to learn how to avoid unpleasant realities. We create environments that shield us from the truth. The prophet Isaiah describes the people of Israel as those "who say to the seers, 'Do not see'; and to the prophets, 'Do not prophesy to us what is right; speak to us smooth things, prophesy illusions'" (Isa. 30:10).

We'll do virtually anything to keep from admitting that our synthetic world is falling apart. Consider just a few of our classic avoidances.

We avoid illness. Susan Sontag once wrote, "Illness is the night-side of life, a more onerous citizenship. Everyone who is born holds dual citizenship, in the kingdom of the well and in the kingdom of the sick. Although we prefer to use only the good passport, sooner or later each of us is obliged, at least for a spell, to identify ourselves as citizens of the other place."[4]

The health-obsessed are taking their vitamins, giving up tobacco, getting their regular exercise, and eating their nonfat, additive-free foods—all to avoid the "more onerous citizenship" of the ill. Many others who follow the opposite course by abusing their bodies refuse to face the truth of the damage their self-indulgence is causing. Either way, we think we're avoiding illness either by preventing it or by ignoring it. Illness is a threat to our happiness.

We avoid pain for the same reason. Surgeon Paul Brand moved to the United States a few years ago. He reports,

> I encountered a society that seeks to avoid pain at all costs. Patients lived at a greater comfort level than any I had previously treated, but they seemed far less equipped to handle suffering and far more traumatized by it. Pain relief in the United States is now [1993] a $63 billion-a-year industry, and television commercials proclaim better and faster pain remedies. One ad slogan bluntly declares, "I haven't got time for the pain."[5]

Brand speaks of a "culture of complaint" in which people are "more liable to whine about a problem or file a lawsuit than to strive to overcome it." The idea that anything good or redemptive can come out of our own pain and suffering, or that our pain must be experienced in order for us to learn the lessons it might be teaching us, is foreign to this culture, even antithetical to it. So we spend billions of dollars annually to find more effective ways to eliminate pain and successfully market the new discoveries, and tens of billions to buy these better ways to keep from hurting. We buy symptom treatment so we won't have to face the suffering that real healing always entails or address the real issues of our broken lives. We're addicted to the easiest possible cure. Pain must be avoided at all costs. The terrible deception in this strategy is the expectation that the elimination of pain will bring happiness. But it never does.

THE CURSE OF AGING AND DEATH

Illness and pain, however, are not all we work to avoid; we also try to escape the reality of growing old. The cult of youth makes a curse of old age. Advertisements lure us with the message that we don't need to appear or act old if their product is applied. One ad from many years ago showed a mother and her adult daughter and asked, "Can you tell which one is the mother?" Presumably, the use of the product being marketed prevented, or at least seriously impeded, aging. People are sometimes regarded in the way we look upon old machinery: no longer useful or productive and ready to be retired out of service. How about a nice retirement community (where they can be segregated from the rest of us and not bother us with the reminder that we, too, will grow old). We see growing old as happiness slipping through our fingers, as the increase of illness, pain, and suffering—and worst of all, as the journey toward death.

The culture of avoidance, above all, tries to shield us from death, which it sees as the enemy of happiness. Death is the final destination of sickness and suffering, of disability and aging, of everything that thwarts our happiness. We invent a language of euphemisms so that we can speak of it as if it were not real. For example, we might say someone has "passed on" or "left us," as if he or she had just decided to take a trip; it sounds less blunt and brutal. This is just about the best we can do when we've spent our lives keeping sufficiently busy in our pursuit of happiness, failing to prepare ourselves for the deaths of those we love—as well as our own.

Avoid. At all costs, avoid. Make these unpleasantries seem nonexistent, or at least far removed, something we need not deal with *now*. Be happy. Be healthy, pain-free, and youthful; and live as if earthly life never comes to an end.

THE CULTURE OF FORGETFULNESS

Avoid thinking about suffering and death long enough, and you'll forget. You'll create an artificial world of happiness and forget the real world, where joy is waiting to overtake us. The real world is a courageous environment—it includes the unpleasantries that the culture of happiness avoids, because joy confronts the shattering experiences that destroy happiness and embraces the healing and hope that God brings through them.

Clearly, memory is one of God's most wonderful gifts to us. In remembering the events of our past, both pleasant and unpleasant, we call to mind the amazing path God's providence has taken in our lives; we learn from our best moments but especially from our worst, and we honestly claim the whole legacy of our past. Remembering means facing the good and the bad. It means not only affirming the past but also repenting of its sins and receiving the healing of its hurts. It means looking at our past through the eyes of a God who gives us courage. Only God makes it possible for us to remember our past faithfully.

It comes as no surprise, then, that those who pursue happiness begin to forget God. Or at least they begin to reconstruct Him into the idolatrous god of their self-indulgence, the god who will remove all unpleasantness, and particularly the unpleasantness of their unaddressed hurts and sins. If we're to pursue the myth of the happy life, we must forget the true and living God.

The Bible knows all about this conspiracy of forgetfulness. Before they enter the Promised Land, Moses warns the people of Israel not to forget God in their coming prosperity, not to get so caught up in their pursuit of the good life that they forget their true God and the difficult lessons of their past (Deut. 8).

But forget they do. The prophet Hosea speaks of an Israel who "has forgotten his Maker, and built palaces" (8:14). The more the people prospered, the more pagan the places of worship (10:1).[6] Isaiah puts traitorous words in the mouth of unfaithful Judah: "Leave the way, turn aside from the path, let us hear no more about the Holy One of Israel" (30:11).

FACING THE REAL TRUTH

The Holy One of Israel does not allow us to avoid the thorny issues of life. He does not even allow us to avoid tough living. The culture of happiness would have us dwell on "the good life." The culture of holiness would have us dwell on the obedient life. Those who pursue happiness cannot understand the strange gratitude of the psalmist who, on noting the apparent happiness and prosperity of the faithless in contrast to his own precarious situation, sings to God: "You have put gladness in my heart more than when their grain and wine abound" (4:7).

They especially cannot understand someone who could have whatever He wanted freely agreeing to the horror of His own crucifixion, enduring the Cross and disregarding the shame

(Heb. 12:2). They would want to join the crowd at the foot of the Cross and plead the only action their view could allow: "Let him come down from the cross now, and we will believe in him" (Matt. 27:42). Let Him show us the way to the good life. Let Him lead us to prosperity. Let Him make us happy.

And the dying One on the Cross replies with a silent witness louder than thunder: you will find joy when you care about the world with My Father's heart, and when you couldn't care less about your own happiness. The God who let His heart be ripped open for all the world to see, the God who taught us that true joy can exist only where love has been poured out and the terrible moments of life faced head-on invites us to quit faking it, quit chasing after the chimeras of our self-centered happiness, quit protecting the desperate pride of our accomplishments. He invites us to loosen our grip on the good life and allow another kind of prosperity to overtake us. He invites us to let the good life find us. He invites us to humble ourselves and receive a joy given and not gotten.

The God who left His own particular form of the good life behind by incarnating himself, by becoming one of us, became in Jesus "the pioneer and perfecter of our faith" (Heb. 12:2). He did it not by going after an earthly happy life with all the gusto He could muster, but by braving the path of joyful obedience, by facing the tough stuff with the courage of His loving, knowing that this was how joy would find Him. Early on in His ministry, Jesus told His hearers to kiss worry good-bye and not allow the lesser things to become their central concerns: "But strive first for the kingdom of God and his righteousness, and all these things will be given to you as well" (Matt. 6:33).

The fortunes of the kingdom of God are the fortunes of the heart. They are the fortunes of which no adversity can rob us; indeed, they are the fortunes that adversity refines. The fortunes of happiness seekers are the fortunes of unreliable circumstance and forced rewards, and their pursuit can be sustained only through our pretending otherwise.

Jesus invites us to seek His kingdom and righteousness and allow His joy to overtake us. We can abandon the futile pursuit of happiness. Joy is back.

6

Joy in the Public World

Holy hilarity loosens us up and opens us up to the ever-expanding possibilities of God's creativity. Sinful somberness, however, closes us down and pulls us back into an unholy privatism. Without joy, we find ourselves increasingly drawn into a self-centered world.

THE EXPANSION OF PRIVACY

Is our world, in fact, becoming more private? Years ago, sociologist Robert Nesbit wrote about the loss of community in the 20th-century Western world and expressed deep concern over our growing alienation and disconnectedness.[1] The accuracy of his analysis seems to have been proven by social disintegration in the second half of the century. Relationships have become increasingly transient and unsustained. Many of us change jobs and residences frequently, and half of us who marry end up divorcing. The pressures of an ever-changing external and relational world push us further into an internal, private world that we feel we can control. Fear of the future shock around the corner puts us in a retreat mode and lures us into protective privatism: we're not sure we're ready for what may be coming. Our private worlds have become the last resorts of personal protection and security. Sitting in front of our computers and accessing the world, while never having to engage it, is a poignant visual image of our alienation.

Where communities do exist, they all too often seem private, closed, exclusive. It happens from the largest communities to the smallest. Many nations have immigration guidelines that are inconsistently applied in order to keep out "undesirable" applicants. One group of citizens of a nation wants another group expelled, repressed, or if need be, even exterminated. Residents of a neighborhood want to keep certain types of people out. Country clubs, often with sophisticated subtlety, devise means to keep out those who don't meet their approval.

Even the Church can retreat into its private world. My own denomination, The Salvation Army, came into existence during the latter half of the 19th century in order to reach the poorer classes of Britain whom the churches in general were ignoring and against whom social and economic barriers had been erected by church practice and policy. The poor working man needed only to enter a church and look for an unrented seat in the back in order to find out where he stood: it was not on the inside.

A world of threatening change tempts us all to embrace security and preserve and protect our private worlds. Like the dignitaries invited to the great gospel banquet, we allow our private concerns to override the opportunity to enter the inclusive world of the real family of God (Luke 14:16-24). Like the prophet Jonah, we run from our mission to reach out to those who are unlike us or are our enemies. What we're really running from is the startling fact that God loves them as much as He loves us—and wants them included. Too often we have retreated into sinful privatism. In that narrow world we may enjoy a certain smug happiness, but the laughter is shallow and short-lived, because it denies God. Nothing kills joy so much as a private faith.

OUR NEED FOR EACH OTHER

We were not meant to be alone. When we live in ourselves, for ourselves, by ourselves, we are not ourselves; in fact, we deny ourselves. There are deep connections between us that define our humanity, and if we don't make those connections, we shrivel up and die in our isolation.

One need not travel far in Scripture to find this truth firmly established. The creation of the human race is not complete until God makes a second human being. Having almost exhausted himself with an incredible outpouring of creations, He checks himself and studies more closely this one whom He has called man, His crowning achievement. Something important is missing. What is it? Being who He is, it probably does not take God long to figure out what it is. Scripture takes the words right out of His mouth: "It is not good that the man should be alone" (Gen. 2:18).

Preacher-poet John Donne would say that it finally is not possible to deny our connectedness with one another. His familiar words in *Devotions upon Emergent Occasions* are still compelling:

> The church is catholic, universal, so are all her actions. All that she does belongs to all. When she baptizes a child, that action concerns me; for that child is thereby connected to that head which is my head too, and engrafted into the body whereof I am a member. . . . No man is an island entire of itself; every man is a piece of the continent, a part of the main. If a clod be washed away by the sea, Europe is the less, as well as if a promontory were, as well as if a manor of thy friend's or of thine own were. Any man's death diminishes me, because I am involved in mankind; and therefore never send to know for whom the bell tolls; it tolls for thee.

This is not a denial of our unique existence as persons. It is an affirmation of our essential unity as human beings. We are connected.

The public arena is the only real arena of joy. There can be smug happiness, but there can be no private joy. Joy by nature is shared. Rejoicing is a community affair (Rom. 12:15).

JOY IN THE ORDINARY

Let's take a closer look at the public character of joy. First, there is a certain joy in simply *being a part of the ordinary*. Christians believe that the greatest affirmation of ordinary life was God coming to be with us in human flesh: the Incarnation. Of course, God knew that His earthly walk would bring plenty of sorrow, misunderstanding, and persecution and that at the end of that earthly life would be a cruel death. None of this was a surprise. But I think that He also thoroughly enjoyed becoming a part of our ordinary lives. There was surely a twinkle in His fatherly eyes on that Bethlehem birth night. That was the night He enjoyed becoming ordinary.

Some of us have a problem with an ordinary Jesus. We think we have to make Him an exception to everything, keep Him as far removed from the mundane as possible—as if He didn't enjoy taking long walks, relishing a good meal, bouncing laughing children on His knee, sharing warm fellowship and good humor with friends. Our belief in the extraordinariness of Jesus should never be permitted to diminish our appreciation of His "ordinariness." In fact, if we allow ourselves to be completely swept away by the "extraordinariness" and turn our backs on the ordinary Jesus, we miss the whole point of the Incarnation: "He had to become like his brothers and sisters in every respect" (Heb. 2:17) in order to become their high priest and lead them to salvation. The Incarnation was not a grim business, a fretting God gritting His teeth and holding His breath until it was all over. It was God's exciting love mission into our lives, a mission that, to be sure, would often bring deep sorrow and pain but also bring the privileges and pleasures of human existence. The Incarnation embraces all of this and invites us to do the same.

The God who became incarnate in Jesus invites us to follow suit: to enjoy ordinary human life as Jesus did, to leave our fortresses of self-protection and self-righteousness and savor the sweet simplicities of the commonplace, to quit pretending we can be extraordinary people without knowing the blessings and embarrassments of the ordinary. A Christian is someone who accepts Jesus' invitation to enjoy the ordinary.

JOY IN OUR SAMENESS

Jesus also invites us to another public joy: the joy of *being alike*. Notice that He had to become *"like* his brothers and sisters in every respect" (Heb. 2:17, emphasis added). There is a certain encouragement that comes to us when we realize how alike we are. And for the Christian, the fact that Jesus was like us brings an encouragement that knows no bounds.

Like Jesus, we're more alike than we're different. We're absolutely alike in what we require to sustain physical life. We all have the same basic emotional and social needs, though experience and personality influence the intensity and healthiness of their expression. We all, I believe, also have a profound hunger for God. For some it has been suppressed and ignored for so long that they refuse to acknowledge it. Still, the impulse persists in all of us, and it will not completely go away. We're all fundamentally alike.

We're especially encouraged by the likeness of our experiences. To know that others are experiencing what we're experiencing makes us feel connected to them. To know that they've suffered what we're suffering brings deep comfort to us. To share sorrow, to share laughter, because we share the same experiences and insights that come in our life's journey, is the reward of our acknowledged sameness. Without it there is no joy.

Henri Nouwen speaks of the joy of being a member of the human family, of brotherhood and sisterhood with everyone, the joy of solidarity with others. He believes that it is this joy that enables us to face death well. Many have the impression that we go to our graves most happily when we bring with us a life of distinct accomplishments, when we know we have made our individual mark. Then, so this thinking goes, we can rest in peace. Nouwen challenges this claim. He says that we die well, we face death with deepest joy, when we come to it in the poverty of our personal claims and the richness of our solidarity with one another. Death is the discovery of our unity with one another, of our full human togetherness, and therefore of our hope. The place of our utter poverty together becomes the place of our deepest joy. When we recognize that alone we have, and have done, nothing, we are ready to have everything—together. We give up our claims to worthy achievements, and we know that, like all others who have traveled with God, "'tis grace hath bro't me safe thus far, / And grace will lead me home." That is why saints die so beautifully.[2]

JOY IN OUR DIFFERENCES

But that's not all. The family is a group of members who are not only alike but also very different. As important and encouraging as our sameness is, if we were only the same as each other, we could not be a family; we could be only a uniformity. Some churches try to force their members into the same box of belief and behavior, insisting on precision of doctrine and exactitude of practice and allowing for diversity only in the most superficial ways. What they are achieving is as much uniformity as they

possibly can—at the cost of true unity. True Christian unity requires rich diversity. Founded on the common ground of a
shared faith, a biblical worldview, and a radical lifestyle, it encourages as much creativity in the expression of the faith life as is
possible. It celebrates both our profound sameness as God's children *and* our considerable differences.

It would come as no surprise, then, that Jesus also invites us
to the joy of *being different*. He did not try to mold His disciples
into His clones. He invited them to be like Him in their love of
God, of each other, and of the world—and to be different in their
personalities, their gifts, and the directions their vocations took.
There is no evidence that He wanted to change the individuality
or originality of any person, only the heart. We never see Him
telling Peter that he is far too passionate, only that his heart
would need forgiveness (Luke 22:31-32). We never see Him
looking down at Matthew the tax collector for his great skill in
(and probably enjoyment of) financial affairs; He simply told him
to follow (Matt. 9:9). He certainly did not suggest to Martha that
her love of domestic work and her skills in behind-the-scene
household management were not important in the life of God's
people. (What would we do without Marthas? Life would be
chaos!) He only asked her not to be distracted by her managerial
duties and miss His presence (Luke 10:38-42). Jesus appreciates
our differences. After all, His Father is responsible for them!

The Bible's story of the first human encounter has an atmosphere of awe and mystery about it. You have to read between the
lines a bit, and you have to project yourself into that scene and
imagine what that first meeting of the first two people would be
like. When Adam glances at Eve for the first time, there is both
recognition and wonder. He can only say, "This at last . . ." (Gen.
2:23). He recognizes a much-longed-for fellow human being,
someone who is like him. But he also sees someone who is dis-
tinctly different; he sees unlikeness. The obvious difference, of
course, is sexual, but this encounter is also a parable of all human
encounters—there is always both likeness and difference. Of
course, Genesis (2:18-25) speaks of such interaction in a prefallen
state. Here, in the meeting of two who are very different, they
"were not ashamed" (v. 25). They fully accepted their differences.

The more private our worlds, the more is our shame and our

fear of self-disclosure, and the greater our difficulty with someone else's differences. The more public our worlds—"public" in the sense of making genuine connections and risking deeper relationships—the greater our comfort with our own differences and with those of others. Isolation makes us ashamed of ourselves and of each other. It is the state into which our sin draws us. Here we cannot celebrate our differences—we hide them in embarrassment; we protect them (Gen. 3:10). In our world of self-protection, we can no longer enjoy our delightful individuality. Good fun becomes a thing of the past (vv. 16-19). Laughter is lost.

Our laughter celebrates our differences. If we weren't different, we wouldn't laugh; sameness is dull. It is no coincidence that we even laugh differently. If you were present at a Needham family gathering and we were laughing, as we often are, you would observe great variances in our laughter. Keitha, my wife, a singer and a social butterfly, would laugh loudly with proper breath support, and her laughter would be like powerful tentacles of interaction and influence, impossible to miss and hard to resist as they drew you in. Heather, our eldest daughter, more shy than her mother but very focused, would laugh in a very spirited way to put you and herself at ease and strengthen the relationship. Holly, our youngest, would laugh softly, in giggling spurts, as the conversation progressed, but when something struck her as really funny, she would let out a very loud laugh and roll her eyes back to accentuate how unbelievable the situation appeared to her. My mother would laugh very politely, as befits her own gentle reserve, but occasionally she would allow herself to get carried away and surprise even herself—especially when her children or grandchildren goaded her into it. My older brother, Walt, would laugh with a controlled yet earthy chuckle as befits his combination of reserve and hands-on intelligence. My sister, Miriam, would laugh robustly at the comedies of human interaction, about which she is especially perceptive, as these emerged in the conversation. My younger brother, John, would lose complete control of himself in a high-pitched cackle that would overpower us all, even Keitha, persuading us that life is shockingly funny. Never mind how I laugh. You can believe me when I say that these gatherings are a laughing zoo. Our laughter both binds us together and celebrates our differences.

Jesus invites us to enjoy our differences, to honor our diversity. He even tells us that we need not get overly exercised about folk who don't conform to our patterns or who go about things in a misguided way (Mark 9:38-41). What is most important is the intention of our hearts.

Jesus also invites us—indeed, He commands us—to embrace the different facets of being Christian. He honors not only our diversity but also our willingness to be different from the world in values, lifestyle, and mind-set. As Paul wrote, "Do not be conformed to this world, but be transformed by the renewing of your minds, so that you may discern what is the will of God— what is good and acceptable and perfect" (Rom. 12:2).

The apostle Paul, who issues this invitation from the Lord, does not have in mind a willingness to be different in private. He has in mind a willingness to be different in public—both in the Church (12:10, 13, 15) and in the larger public arena (vv. 14, 17-21). In public we discover and affirm our diversity. In public we must be willing to be different. In public we joyfully celebrate the uniqueness of who we are in Christ.

THE JOY OF BEING TOGETHER

But we also celebrate something else in public: we celebrate community. Christ invites us to the joy of *being together*. The trite romantic cliché "We were meant for each other" has a thread of larger truth to it. We, all of us, were meant for each other. It is not good for any of us to be always alone with ourselves; it is depressing and debilitating. We cannot do without one another: utter aloneness is despair.

One of the great deceptions of Western individualism is the myth of self-sufficiency. Men especially are encouraged not to be overly dependent on others. They are to be strong and resourceful, independent and in control of their destinies. The power of the myth is revealed in the kidding from his friends heaped upon the poor soul who relates any incident from his homelife that suggests that his wife might be having her way with him. You can readily recall the kinds of comments that would be forthcoming: "She really has *you* wrapped around her little finger, doesn't she?" and so forth.

The myth of self-sufficiency has been applied almost exclusively to men over recent centuries—until recently. The women's movement, having made a significant contribution toward gender equality, has in some of its expressions unfortunately adopted the same myth for women. Women must be completely self-sufficient, at least as far as men are concerned. It is acceptable to need other women, who are your sisters, but not men, who are somehow not your brothers. This, of course—and unfortunately—is the transference of the idolatrous notion of male self-sufficiency to the opposite sex, where it is equally idolatrous and hurtful.

As we have seen, Scriptures give a very different view of relationships between the sexes. It simply is not good for man and woman to be alone, not to be together either as life partners or as friends.

It is not good for us to be alone as persons. Creation calls us to a life together, and redemption in Christ makes that life possible for us, self-sufficing pretenders that we are. That is why any sign in the Early Church that life together was not working, that it was not joy, warranted serious attention from the leaders. The Corinthian church is one example: unhappy divisions occurred there because members aligned themselves with different leaders and claimed spiritual superiority for their group. Clearly these divisions constituted an attack on the integrity of the one household (temple) of God (1 Cor. 3).

The Philippian church is another example: there enough division had occurred, possibly centering around Euodia and Syntyche (Phil. 4:2-3), to elicit from Paul his most eloquent hymn to humility toward one another, patterned after the utter self-giving humility of Christ (2:1-11). Humility is the glue of genuine togetherness. The way to experience the deep joy of life together is to humble ourselves before one another in the knowledge that what we share is far more important than what divides us.

Something happened during the First World War that illustrates the power of this truth. Allen Satterlee tells the story in his church newsletter:

> August 1914 saw the crushing war machine of the German army rolling into Belgium and France. Overmatched and overwhelmed, the Allied forces finally stopped the Kaiser's juggernaut and World War I settled into the meatgrinder affair of blighted battlefields hemmed in by disease-

filled trenches of men and mud. The Christian nations of Europe vied with one another to find new ways to kill. The airplane, the tank, poison gas, and long-range artillery were all introduced in an effort to destroy more of the enemy. Despite this, the war had settled down to a stalemate, resembling two weary boxers throwing punishing punches but failing to gain the knockout.

The misery was no more apparent than in the front lines, where men much too young faced each other. The weather was particularly brutal, with incessant rains that turned the trenches into swamps, chilled by autumn's winds. It was the very definition of "bleak."

But on Christmas Eve something remarkable happened. A cold front moved in that caused the temperature to drop dramatically. The mud froze, and it was easier to move around. Not only that, the cold made it feel like Christmas.

Along the British lines the soldiers were on alert. Cautioned that the enemy might try to launch an offensive, they saw specks of light across the way. Officers ordered snipers to shoot at the lights, and as they did, the lights went out. But then they were lit again. It was noted that the fire was not behind the enemy trenches where forces would gather before an offensive was launched, but *in* the trenches. A closer look revealed the incredible: the lights were candles. And the candles were on trees. Christmas trees. A German voice cried out in English, "Don't shoot!"

Still uncertain as to the intention of the enemy, the soldiers were now lined up along their trenches, machine guns loaded and rifles pointed. With a mixture of fear and fascination, they waited in silence. Across the battlefield a lone harmonica began to play. As it played, it was joined by voices, a few at first and then more. Though in German, the British knew the English translation:

> *Silent night! holy night!*
> *All is calm, all is bright*
> *Round yon virgin mother and Child.*
> *Holy Infant, so tender and mild,*
> *Sleep in heavenly peace;*
> *Sleep in heavenly peace.*

German soldiers then started moving toward the trenches of the British. Without orders and without thought, the British left their trenches and moved forward as well. In the middle they met and shook hands. Pictures of families were compared. Gifts were exchanged, and the warring troops began singing.

First one would sing in their language, and then the other. A few times they sang the carol together.

Beyond human strategy and understanding, Christ brings peace. Neither war nor misery nor hopelessness is enough to extinguish the Light. In the clenched fist of the Babe of Bethlehem is the power to bring the world to its knees, to bring peace where none existed.[3]

INCLUSIVE TOGETHERNESS

On the stark battlefields of our lives where often we feel so cut off from one another, so threatened by those whose differences have been magnified into danger, the joy of togetherness may still break through if we let it. It happens when we step out of the trenches of our cowering safety because we believe what most people consider to be not worth the risk: that God actually empowers us to come together, as suspicious and untrustworthy as we so often seem to be, and make some kind of community. Those who take this risk will, in one way or another, find the joy of being together.

It is not a smug togetherness, nor an exclusive affiliation. The joy of being together must never degenerate into the grimness of collective narrow-mindedness. Christ invites us to share the joy of *being inclusive*. The parties of the kingdom of God are very public, and since everyone is invited, much of the fun is seeing who shows up. Of course, we all need our small group— we need an intimate community of trustworthy and trusted friends with whom we can unburden ourselves and openly share our hearts. We need a support group or network. But we also need to be part of a larger community with no boundaries other than the love of God, a community for anyone who wants to give that love a try. Anyone. Try to predict who shows up to join, and you'll be stumped time and time again. You just never know.

That is the beautiful thing about this off-balance Kingdom:

you can't keep people out. God keeps letting them in and making them His sons and daughters. And we have to keep adjusting to diversity within and expanding horizons without. Either we resist this inclusiveness and sulk like Jonah, or we go with it and scour the streets like Jesus. Guess which one is fun. Christian caring is not a private affair. Yes, we must take care of ourselves; self-neglect and self-abuse damage our wholeness. Yes, we must care for those we are closest to; neglect of our loved ones deprives them and diminishes us. But our care must also go public, or it is only self-serving. We must love those who may well not love us in return. We must give ourselves to those who can give us nothing. We must, incredibly, love as God does.

This is precisely what holiness is. Christ calls us to "be imitators of God, as beloved children, and [to] live in love, as Christ loved us and gave himself up for us, a fragrant offering and sacrifice to God" (Eph. 5:1-2).

FAITH MADE EFFECTIVE THROUGH LOVE

We come to Christ through faith, but that faith is made effective through love (Gal. 5:6). When we have arrived at faith, when we get to the place in which we trust God, we're at the starting line, not the finish line. The purpose of faith is to make the journey possible, to bring us into the realm of God's grace and mercy so that we have the self-confidence and self-acceptance to love as He loved us. Love is the thing. It is faith gone public. It is the holy life.

Holiness may be studied and sharpened in solitude and reflection; but it is lived out in public. As we were not meant to be alone, so the way we were meant to live (the holy life) is interactive. As our family was meant to be as big and varied as the world, so our attitudes and actions were meant to be inclusive.

The gospel is an invitation to live in the public arena and there to have the time of our lives. This has nothing to do with personality, as if the shy person must be left behind. We would be wrong to conclude that just because a person is shy, he or she cannot care deeply and practically, just as we would be wrong to conclude that just because someone is publicly confident and influential, he or she is living in a caring way. The gospel invites us to a life of caring beyond our narrow world, whether we are sociable or shy. It invites us to follow the One who emerged from the obscurity of a Galilean village, became the most controversial figure of first-century Palestine, was lifted up on a Cross for all the world to see, and invited the world to an open victory procession to celebrate what the Cross won and to a banquet prepared for anyone who wants to come—a very public Christ.

A Public Faith

Over 150 years ago in England, the people of God, it seemed, had largely retreated to their private enclaves of narrow, exclusive spirituality. A census taken at midcentury revealed that 90 percent of the population never darkened the doors of a place of worship. Fortunately there were some Christian groups who were the exception, providing notable instances of outreach to a suffering populace.

One of them was The Salvation Army. When this group started appearing in the 1870s, the people of Britain were shocked. The Salvationists were so, well, *public*. They marched through the streets, threw aside ecclesiastical terminology, adopted the language of the common people, embraced the culture of the working classes, and crusaded and cared for the poor. It was all too public to be avoided. These brazen fanatics would have to be attacked. And they were—physically by organized bands of ruffians who were incited by pub owners and by police who blamed the Salvationists for inciting public disorder and verbally by the secular newspapers as well as the church press. But the Army would not go away.

Oddly enough, one of its strongest supporters was George Bernard Shaw. Shaw wrote of the Army's emergence:

> In the poorest corner of this soul-destroying Christendom vitality suddenly begins to germinate again. Joyousness, a sacred gift long dethroned by the hellish laughter of derision and obscenity, rises like a flood miraculously out of the fetid dust and mud of the slums; rousing marches and impetuous dithyrambs rise to the heavens from people among whom the depressing noise called "sacred music" is a standing joke; a flag with blood and fire on it is unfurled, not in murderous rancour, but because fire is beautiful and blood is vital and splendid red; fear, which we flatter by

calling self, vanishes; and transfigured men and women carry their Gospel through a transfigured world.[4]

The Church is God's army invading the world with public faith and passionate love, connecting the disconnected, restoring the lost, healing the broken, reuniting the global family of God. It is the most joyful undertaking on this planet.

7
꙳

Joy Restored: A Banquet Invitation

Consider the mission of Jesus to a world lying in the stupor of "solemn stillness." How was Jesus to challenge this dark, deadly spiritual sleep called sin? He would do it by flooding our dinginess with His own luminosity. He, the Light of the World (John 8:12), would introduce the light of God's new age, the light Isaiah saw when he issued his summons to the new messianic kingdom: "O dwellers in the dust, awake and sing for joy! For your dew is a radiant dew, and the earth will give birth to those long dead" (Isa. 26:19).

The apostle Paul repeats the same summons, only he puts Christ at the center of it: "Sleeper, awake! Rise from the dead, and Christ will shine on you" (Eph. 5:14). It is now time to let the light awaken us to joy.

THE BANQUET HALL

Picture an immense room flooded with light. A magnificent banquet is set. The guests have arrived and are having a hilariously good time. The air is suffused with joy. You can tell that they are all grateful to be there, and the host could not be happier that they have come.

This was one of Jesus' favorite ways to frame His mission. He came to call the world to His kingdom banquet. He came to awaken us from the dark sleep of our sin and invite us to the brightly lit room of His messianic feast. We love the story He told that began, "Someone gave a great dinner and invited many" (Luke 14:16). Jesus came to invite us to a meal, to let the good times roll, to bring laughter back—to give us back our lost joy.

If sin means anything, it certainly means joy lost. King David lost his joy when he committed adultery and engineered a murder, and when he prays for restoration, he asks that along with divine forgiveness and cleansing he would have the joy of God's salvation restored to him (Ps. 51:12). Should we be surprised that the New Testament begins with the announcement that the joy has returned? Angels sing about "good news of great joy" (Luke 2:10), and seers from the East become "overwhelmed with joy" just at the sight of the natal star (Matt. 2:10). Joy is about to return for good.

The gospel is the good news of *joy given*. Isaiah sees the messianic King as one who will increase the nation's joy (9:3). The apostle Paul reminds a congregation caught up in petty feuding over meat offered to idols that "the kingdom of God is . . . righteousness and peace and joy in the Holy Spirit" (Rom. 14:17). Joy is God's gift—not a token gift, but a transforming gift. As noted earlier, in Botticelli's the *Mystic Nativity,* the whole universe seems to be dancing, except the demons, who are scampering as quickly as possible to escape the celebration—and their doom. In Piero della Francesca's Nativity scene, the donkey is laughing. Indeed, this somber world will never be the same.

SILENT GIFT

To be sure, those not in immediate proximity to the event are unaware of what happens that night, and the handful who witness it certainly don't grasp its full significance. One could almost say that the Savior is smuggled in, largely unnoticed. There's no earthshaking announcement invading every corner of the globe, no blaring trumpets awakening everyone from sleep or shaking them out of their distractions. Instead, said Phillips Brooks,

> *How silently, how silently*
> *The wondrous gift is giv'n!*
> *So God imparts to human hearts*
> *The blessings of his heav'n.*

No ear may hear His coming;
But in this world of sin,
Where meek souls will receive Him still,
The dear Christ enters in.

The silent gift, the Child of joy, is cradled in the affirming love of chosen parents. During the growing-up years, unnoticed by the rest of the world, He learns the ways of His Heavenly Father in the ways of His earthly family. He learns the simple delights of family fellowship.

AVID BANQUETER

High on the list of delights are the family gatherings, the special meals that often include friends and occasionally even a stranger or two, as obedience to the law of hospitality requires. The Child never forgets the warmth and acceptance of those gatherings.

In fact, the memories of banquets capture His mind—and His actions as well. He becomes an avid banqueter! As a grown man on a mission, He rarely if ever turns down an invitation to feast or banquet, and He may even have crashed a party or two. The scribes and Pharisees are scandalized by such behavior from someone so many consider to be a "religious leader." At least John the Baptist, they say, with all his faults got it right by teaching his disciples to fast and pray. Your disciples, Jesus, seem to be majoring in eating and drinking. What kind of example is *that*?

Jesus has an answer for them: "You cannot make wedding guests fast while the bridegroom is with them, can you?" (Luke 5:34). As important as fasting and praying are, when God calls us to supper, when the banquet invitation is issued, when the table of fellowship and fun is spread, it is not time to withdraw—it is time to come on in!

This is not an invitation to indulgence and excess. Jesus' detractors try to read it that way, accusing Him of gluttony and excessive drinking (Matt. 11:19; Luke 7:34). They miss the point. The point is that the Bridegroom from God has come, and the wedding feast of the kingdom of God is ready. Gone are the somber duties of religion. Gone is the guilt of not measuring up to expectations beyond a sinner's grasp. Gone is a holiness for which only a select few qualify. Here to stay is the Bridegroom, the Party Host, the Joy-bringer, illumining the banquet hall with His countenance and shocking us with a holiness that is as appealing as it is authentic.

Two Mountains

This all brings us to the writer to the Hebrews, who is more than ready to drive the nails into the coffin of the somber legalisms and dread of most religions. Speaking to those who before Christ knew only the frustrations and failures of trying to measure up and please God with good behavior, he draws a stark contrast. Their lives had been lived at the foot of foreboding Mount Sinai, the birthplace of the religion of Law and duty. It was a place associated with "a blazing fire, and darkness, and gloom, and a tempest" (12:18). The air around it was pierced with "the sound of a trumpet, and a voice whose words made the hearers beg that not another word be spoken to them" (v. 19). It was a place before which even Moses said, "I tremble with fear" (v. 21). The good news is that they, the followers of Christ, have moved and now live elsewhere. They live in grace. They live at the foot of Mount Zion, and it has a completely different feel to it: "But you have come to Mount Zion and to the city of the living God, the heavenly Jerusalem, and to innumerable angels in festal gathering, and to the assembly of the firstborn who are enrolled in heaven" (vv. 22-23).

We cannot have it both ways. We cannot live at the foot of Mount Sinai and the foot of Mount Zion at the same time. We cannot live under the clouds of the sinful failure and the sunshine of liberating grace at the same time. Old wineskins will not hold the new wine (Luke 5:37). The despairing ways of our past must give way to the delightful pleasures of a new life. The banquet table of the kingdom of God has been prepared.

A Table Spread

All that is required is that we come to the table, that we accept the invitation to the banquet. All we must do is to give up the thousand and one excuses for declining—and just come. Choose a joyous life launched in the bright banquet hall where doors to the future are open. Jesus has brought joy, and He has invited us all to have it.

What we must do is *claim* it. We must accept the summons. We must show up at the feast. We must be prepared for the time of our lives. Poet George Herbert describes the surprise that awaits us:

Love bade me welcome; yet my soul drew back,
    Guilty of dust and sin.
But quick-ey'd Love, observing me grow slack
    From my first entrance in,
Drew nearer to me, sweetly questioning
    If I lacked any thing.
"A guest," I answer'd, "worthy to be here."
    Love said, "You shall be he."
"I the unkind, ungrateful? Ah my dear,
    I cannot look on thee."
Love took my hand, and smiling did reply,
    "Who made the eyes but I?"
"Truth Lord, but I have marr'd them; let my shame
    Go where it doth deserve."
"And know you not," says Love, "who bore the blame?"
    "My dear, then I will serve."
"You must sit down," says Love, "and taste the meat."
    So I did sit and eat.[1]

Your complete and utter unworthiness cannot keep you out: the Host has acquired a blind spot and cannot see it. You cannot even earn a place by waiting on tables: the Host will have none of it—He will have you as His cherished guest. The gospel invitation is for those who bring nothing but themselves, and the delight of their hearts is the improbable reality of their inclusion. This they have dared to claim.

PENITENCE

But they have claimed their inclusion on their knees. The overwhelming fact of this privilege gives us no cause for pride, only penitence. But please let us be clear. The penitence we are talking about is the outcome of affirmation, not self-loathing. We do not become penitent because we feel worthless; we become penitent because we are treated as if we were worthy. The Host considers us worthy, and shaken by His opinion, we become aware of how unworthily we have been thinking and living. Through His gracious invitation, we begin to see how much better we are than we ever thought or acted, and so we're shattered by the realization that we have missed the mark so badly. This "shattering," if you will, becomes the sacrifice we bring to our restoration. David knew this quite well: "The sacrifice acceptable to God is a broken spirit; a broken and contrite heart, O God, you will not despise" (Ps. 51:17).

The way to joy is not easy or painless. It is through brokenness. God in Christ welcomes us home as if we were the most important persons in His life, and He holds a banquet in our honor. If that doesn't bring us to our knees, I don't know what will—especially when we realize that the cost for all this was as incalculable as God giving His life on a Cross. There on our knees, joy and sorrow comingle. This is penitence, and this is the way joy begins—the only way.

Now the bright lights of the banquet feast lie before us. We enter the luminous hall. We feast in the light.

LIGHT WALK

We also walk in it. The beaming message of the gospel is not just an invitation to bask in banquet light but also a summons to live well in its radiance. Our Host intends not only that we sit at His table but also that we walk in His light, live in loving fellowship with one another, and experience cleansing from all sin (1 John 1:5-9). We have been invited to the table of holiness. Christ calls us to good times *and* good living. It's never one without the other.

We are all too ready to receive the promising seed of good news. But allowing it to take deep root and grow us into something quite better than we are is often not to our liking. Some might prefer a shallow quick fix, plenty of fun without the pain of changing. Like the rocky ground in Jesus' parable of the sower, they "immediately receive it [the gospel] with joy. But they have no root, and endure only for a while" (Mark 4:16-17).

The banquet is not for those who only want to be included. It is for those who also want to become who they are, those who want to recover the deeply tarnished image of God in their lives, those who want to live out their true humanity and be what they were meant to be—in short, those who want to be holy.

This, by the way, is the only pursuit that brings real joy. The prophet Isaiah knew this centuries before Christ. When he spoke of "the ransomed of the LORD" returning to Zion with singing and with everlasting joy on their heads (Isa. 35:10), he first made clear that the highway they would be traveling on would be called "the Holy Way" and that the unclean would not be traveling on it (v. 8). Plenty of hilarity all right, but grounded in the way of holiness—holy hilarity, the joy of the pure in heart, the sheer pleasure of walking in the light.

GOOD COMPANY

The joy is found also in the good company. We don't banquet alone. Around us are other redeemed sinners. What's more, they're more than company: they've become our brothers and sisters, and we can't escape the fact. They're here to stay.

For many, it seems, this is where the gospel meal goes bad; this is where the party fizzles. We're ever so glad about being included in the Kingdom banquet. We're thrilled that the Host has put our names on the eternal guest list. But we may not like the idea that everyone in the huge banquet hall is now close family. We may not relish sharing the table permanently with persons who don't pass our preference test.

But the banquet hall of the Kingdom is very brightly lit. There are no dark corners or hidden adjoining rooms. Every face can be seen. Every person is there to be taken seriously. Everyone present is family; everyone is loved. And the Host never stops reminding His family, "This is my commandment, that you love one another as I have loved you" (John 15:12). When we fail to take this commandment seriously, when we forget that love is the only debt we owe one another (Rom. 13:8), our spiritual vision dims, and all around us seems darkness. Undoubtedly the apostle John had seen this happen more than once. He wrote, "Whoever says, 'I am in the light,' while hating a brother or sister, is still in the darkness." Furthermore, writes John, he or she "does not know the way to go, because the darkness has brought on blindness" (1 John 2:9, 11).

LIGHT AND LOVE

John has a wonderful way of bringing light and love together. To love someone, we must somehow see him or her. We can't genuinely love people in general—we can love them only in particular. We must let the light shine on their faces and see them for who they are. The light invites us to know them—so that we can love them. Therefore, if (for whatever reason) we are afraid to love, we choose a certain darkness. We choose not to see, not to know, and we live "still in the darkness."

It is a tragedy that so many who enter the Lord's banquet hall start acting as if the lights aren't really on. Perhaps their eyes have atrophied in the darkness they have left. Their vision is severely limited. They are not yet ready to take in the whole banquet crowd, to see the whole colorful lot and learn to love them for who they are and for what they're becoming. Instead, they seek out a very small private room. They claim only a secret joy, which, like a rope of sand, disappears in their hands. The gospel feast is for those who are willing to see by the light of God's inclusive love.

You see, once we get used to it, this banquet hall fellowship can become fun. And we can begin to feel quite cozy and comfortable in it.

INVITATIONS

But something disturbing invariably happens later during the feast. The Host stands to His feet and calls us to order. Then He shocks us: He tells us to leave.

"Wait a minute! We've been having a terrific time. We've even been getting used to each other. And, Jesus—You're really quite a Host! Why are You breaking up the party? Why are You sending us away?"

Patiently He waits for us to finish expressing our puzzlement. Then He smiles and says, "Have you noticed how big this banquet hall is? Not only does it *look* big, but it's even bigger than it looks. In fact, it can hold as many as want to come in. Why do you think I built it that way?"

Somewhat sheepishly we say, "Uh—because You want a lot more in?"

"Actually," He says, "I want everyone in, but they must *want* in, must want to sit at My table. And they need to be invited."

"So how does all that happen?" we ask, suspecting by now that we're going to be given some role in publicizing the party and issuing the invitations.

"I'm glad you asked," He says with a smile. "It happens by My Spirit, who's out there at work everywhere. But I have decided that, by far, the best way for My Spirit to be convincing and inviting is for His message to be carried in flesh and blood— that's you. The invitation has to come to them in ways they can see, hear, and touch. You are those ways. You are My hilarious saints spilling the overflow of Kingdom joy everywhere you are, getting noticed without trying to, drawing people to a life they deeply long for because it's what they were made for, loving people because they're your long-lost brothers and sisters who belong in your Father's kingdom and have a place waiting for them at the banquet table. You're the best and most convincing way I have to invite My lost people to the banquet. That's why I'm sending you out."

REJECTIONS

Then comes a thoughtful pause. He goes on: "You also need to be aware that your job will sometimes be very tough. Some of My lost people have allowed themselves to get so used to the dark alleys of their shameful sin that they refuse to acknowledge their longing for a luminous place where they have nothing to hide. Some have rejected love and are practicing hate. Still others have become prisoners of their own fear of life. And a very large number have simply settled into a godless complacency and don't want to be disturbed with any invitations to leave their ruts and embark on a new course.

"What you need to know is that these folks will sometimes respond to you in very adverse ways. You'll experience suffering in one form or another. That's how it was when I walked the earth. In fact, it seemed that every time I left one of those delightful banquet meals or lively parties, there was someone— usually more than one—waiting to give Me a very tough time. But, then, I knew it would be that way; the Father had told Me. And, of course, the last time I left the banquet hall, a cross was waiting for Me."

We wonder: How did we get from a banquet to a cross? We thought this was all about good times and fellowship with the King of Kings. We know we must bring our own personal brokenness. And we know that we must welcome to the Kingdom banquet whoever comes. But now the Host is asking us to do more than welcome visitors: He's asking us to leave the banquet hall between meals and scatter ourselves over the community to publicize the banquet and issue the invitations. He's even asking us, in a way, to "take the meal with us," to practice the table manners of the Kingdom out there, to live in the light, to treat every person as a dear brother or sister.

Reading our thoughts, the Host says, "You're beginning to get it. Now, you must understand that what I am asking of you is totally inappropriate behavior in the world. It does not fit, and many people won't like it. If they were to allow it, it would call into question their own way of life. So they'll either ignore you or try to break you. Both are painful. But if you consult the Book, you'll find that I said to My very first disciples, 'In the world you will have trouble' [John 16:33, NEB]. You will have trouble because I am calling you to inappropriate behavior, trouble because you'll break convention by not bowing to the power structures and their definitions of importance, trouble because you'll follow a love that includes the least desirable and the most undeserving, trouble because, well, the mission to which I call a person turns the social order on its stuffy head."

A COMMISSION

We begin to see the whole picture, that this is the way it is in the Kingdom in which our Host invites us to participate. We who come to the dinner leave with a commission, and the commission gives us permission to live, and power to love, in a radical way. And strange as it may seem, that's the way to joy. There is no joy nurtured in the seclusion of the Kingdom banquet hall; there is no private joy in the family of God. We, the saints of God, dance our way into the world, proving the joy that endures all things as we invite everyone to the Kingdom party. Nothing can stop us, and we'll stop at nothing, because the Host says, "Take courage; I have conquered the world!" (John 16:33)—and we're crazy enough to believe Him.

So there you have it. The gospel is a wide-open invitation to the family banquet. Discipleship is how you live as a family member. And mission is recruiting for the family by issuing personal invitations and living the family life outside the family, whatever the cost.

This, and this alone, is the way to joy. This is what the hilarious saints of God believe, and this is how they live their lives. Theirs is an ever-expanding banquet hall with places of honor for the unhonored and acts of love for the unloved. Perhaps one of the best descriptions of this strange feast is found in the table grace associated with Brigid, an amazing Celtic saint of centuries ago:

> *I should like a great lake of finest ale*
> *For the King of kings.*
> *I should like a table of the choicest food*
> *For the family of heaven.*
> *Let the ale be made from the fruits of faith,*
> *And the food be forgiving love.*
>
> *I should welcome the poor to my feast,*
> *For they are God's children.*
> *I should welcome the sick to my feast,*
> *For they are God's joy.*
> *Let the poor sit with Jesus at the highest place,*
> *And the sick dance with the angels.*
>
> *God bless the poor,*
> *God bless the sick,*
> *And bless our human race.*
> *God bless our food,*
> *God bless our drink,*
> *All homes, O God, embrace.*[2]

Part 3

Hilarity
in the Church

8
⁂

Good Reason No. 1:
A Liberating Forgiveness

The Church is the group of people who love God and want to enjoy Him forever. As lovers do, of course, God and they like to spend time laughing together. Their living is permeated with joy, their holiness with hilarity. After all, they have plenty to rejoice over.

But even Christians sometimes lose the joy and miss the laughter. Their troubles *weigh* them down, their self-doubts *keep* them down, or their friends *let* them down. It all conspires to rob them of their joy. The laughter of heaven seems to recede.

When this happens, it's time for a reality check. (Despair—remember—is the fruit of deception; joy is the fruit of truth.) We have every good reason to rejoice and be exceedingly glad. In these final seven chapters, I'll be inviting you to consider them and treasure them. The joy of the Lord is here to stay.

Let's begin with forgiveness. Forgiveness is best captured in a story Jesus told in Luke 15:11-32. A young man, broken and penniless, makes his way home after a period of self-indulgence, squandering, and profligacy. He's returning to his father, the one on whom he had earlier turned his back and from whom he had insensitively demanded his inheritance. He doesn't expect forgiveness and certainly doesn't deserve it. He's sure he has forfeited his status as a family member; the most he can hope for is a position on the hired staff.

As he approaches the homestead, he suddenly notices that someone is running toward him. He's amazed to discover that it's his father. Is he in a hurry to pummel him with wrath and turn him away forever? Who could blame him if he did? He had hurt his father deeply.

What the father does when he draws near has nothing to do with the usual scripts of retribution. It is the script of a heart that loves no matter what. The prodigal son begins his confession (I picture him on his knees), but his father doesn't let him finish.

Forgiveness isn't earned—it's given. The Church is a fellowship of forgiven prodigals.

FORGIVEN SINNERS

Forgiveness, of course, is a gift to be accepted on our knees in penitence and quiet gratitude. But it's also a shocker—not because we have gotten away with something (we haven't), but because even though He knows how we have failed Him, He holds no grudge against us; He exacts no compensation; He demands no punishment. Instead, He says, "I have taken care of your past and am ready to leave it behind. If you can go with Me on this, I have a very new life for you."

In Ps. 139 David speaks of a God who is inescapable in every way. It's embarrassing enough that this unrelenting "hound of heaven" sees the psalmist's every action, but it's devastating that He sees his heart. David has learned that there are no places where we can harbor and protect our deepest and most damaging secrets. But this is not the shocker. It's that God says we can be in that place of vulnerability without fear that He will harm us for it, that we can confess our sin and be forgiven, that God sees us as we are and still loves us. So David turns this stunning reality into a prayer, actually pleading with God to do what He does anyway: know him inside and out: "Search me, O God, and know my heart; test me and know my thoughts. See if there is any wicked way in me, and lead me in the way everlasting" (Ps. 139:23-24).

Amazing! We willingly expose ourselves to God and know that He will love us still. There is only one possible explanation for such insanity, and it is this: *God's forgiveness is real.*

COUNTERFEIT CONFESSIONS

It's tragic that all too often burdened people seek forgiveness without finding it. Confession has become trendy these days, and we're being inundated by parodies of self-exposure. Public "purging" has almost become a national pastime in some countries where many are hungry for some release from their boredom. More and more people are parading their private problems and secret sins before television cameras for the thrill of massive exposure and notoriety (and perhaps a sizable bit of pocket money). Then almost everyone gets a shot at self-righteous condemnation, cheap affirmation, or easy prescription: the show host, the summoned experts, the studio audience, and those who may call in. The idea, of course, is to bring such "honesty" to everyone except God, the One who knows what honesty truly is. Perhaps the players secretly suspect that God won't play around with the sin and exploit it as they do.

They're correct. Instead, seeing the sin in all its magnitude and meaning, God will always forgive the sinner and give him or her a new life. It's a shame that such good news and such a liberating outcome is not what the producers want. It's a shame that in many cases personal exposure has become a cheap, titillating, self-serving display by those who have no intention of changing. It's a shame that such souls can't find forgiveness because their self-exposure is a sham, a parody of honest confession, a false search for mercy without exposure to a merciful God. They don't know what the psalmist knows: that forgiveness is an act of God, a loving God who takes us as we are and gives us what we never dreamed we could have.

THE ECSTASY OF PARDON

No wonder God's forgiveness sends David into ecstasy. No wonder he blurts out, "Happy are those whose transgression is forgiven, whose sin is covered. Happy are those to whom the LORD imputes no iniquity" (Ps. 32:1-2).

If ever a person needed forgiveness, David did. If ever an individual needed to throw himself on God's mercy, he did—and that's precisely what we see him doing: "Then I acknowledged my sin to you, and I did not hide my iniquity; I said, 'I will confess my transgressions to the LORD,' and you forgave the guilt of my sin" (v. 5).

Surprisingly, David is now counted among the righteous. He can hardly believe it; he's dumbfounded. But he has the presence of mind to do what any good psalmist would do on such an occasion: he musters the congregation of forgiven saints and leads them in a verse. The words spring from his liberated soul: "Be glad in the LORD and rejoice, O righteous, and shout for joy, all you upright in heart" (v. 11).

THE PERSON WHO PARDONS

Many years later, the forgiving heart of God takes the form of Jesus of Nazareth. The world of that day is conjuring up all kinds of palpable rites and rituals in order to make the removal of their guilt seem concrete and personal, but these contrived appeasements simply will not do. Performances can bring catharsis, but not forgiveness: only a *person* can forgive a person.

If anyone had an accumulated glut of sin to deal with, it was the apostle Paul. In the name of religion he committed horrible crimes against humanity. Underneath the veneer of uprightness, he carried an incredibly heavy burden of guilt. One day he carried that load in his heart as he traveled to Damascus, and out of nowhere the forgiving Person appeared and gave Paul the shattering news that he was indeed a sinner and that all his sin against others had also been sin against Him (Acts 9:1-5).

Then the miracle happened: the Lord forgave Paul. A life was turned around. Forgiven, Paul would never be the same, and he would never forget that every remaining day of his life was to be lived under the banner of forgiveness. Halfway through his greatest letter preserved in Scripture, he declared, "There is therefore now no condemnation for those who are in Christ Jesus" (Rom. 8:1). No condemnation for the worst sinner forgiven! Shocking—but true.

No wonder the Church sings! People who can leave behind the failures and wrongs of their past make the music of liberation. They have grieved over their sins, but their grief has been what Paul calls "godly" rather than "worldly." "Godly grief," he wrote, "produces a repentance that leads to salvation and brings no regret, but worldly grief produces death" (2 Cor. 7:10). There is a grieving without hope: it is a mourning for our sins without a Person to forgive them. But there is a good grief: it is a mourning in true sorrow in the presence of a generous forgiveness. Such forgiveness is God's gift to us, setting us on our way with a song in our hearts and making us that remarkable community that is His Church: a hilarious fellowship of forgiven people.

A FORGIVING FELLOWSHIP

But there's still another reason for the joy. We find another side to this state of being forgiven, and if that side lies unexposed and undeveloped, the experience of forgiveness becomes mere self-indulgence. "Forgiven-ness" is not God's gift to those who want an out for themselves, a way to escape the consequences of their conceit. It's the way in to a life turned outward, a way to embrace the truly hilarious freedom of grace by allowing "forgiven-ness" to become "forgiving-ness."

The Church is a hilarious fellowship of forgiving people. Now, please: let's not make this into something sweet and pretty—you know, "those precious Christians who are so understanding. Aren't they nice?" The truth of the matter is that "forgiving-ness" usually does not fit well and is not appreciated in a world that wants to pretend that everyone should get his or her "due." Perform an act of forgiveness toward someone, and you can be sure there will be someone else around who resents it and says silently, if not aloud, "That person should have gotten what was coming to him"—never thinking for one moment that *forgiveness* was what he had coming. We live in a get-even world that has little time or tolerance for "forgiving-ness."

Of course, "getting even" really is not that at all. No one gets even to get even. You get even to have an advantage, to go the other person one better, to stay on top of the contest of pain infliction. You get even to make the other person feel bad so that you can feel good. It's all very calculated behavior, a careful controlling of one's hurt or defeat at the hands of someone else and a secret strategizing to inflict even more on the perceived persecutor. It is perfectly summed up in the motto "Don't get mad. Get even!" What a sad way to spend one's life!

Now there are certain principles of equity by which every community must live. There must be laws, rules, and regulations that set the limits on what you can do to other people and what they can do to you, as well as reciprocal penalties that are administered when someone oversteps the lines. The followers of Christ are enjoined to abide by the rules (Rom. 13:1-7), except when doing so would compromise their obedience to God (Acts 5:29). They are not given a license to except themselves or to protect the guilty. They must abide by laws that aim at equity and fairness.

But they are also given a command to forgive: "Just as the Lord has forgiven you, so you also must forgive" (Col. 3:13). They are given a prayer that permanently binds "forgiven-ness" and "forgiving-ness": "And forgive us our debts, as we also have forgiven our debtors. . . . For if you forgive others their trespasses, your heavenly Father will also forgive you" (Matt. 6:12, 14). And they are given the freedom of tenderheartedness, the freedom to "put away . . . bitterness and wrath and anger and wrangling and slander" (Eph. 4:31) and all forms of "get-evenness" and to become "imitators of God" (5:1). Imitators of God—how presumptuous this seems! Actually, the opposite is the case. Sin is putting ourselves in the place of God, acting as if we *were* God. Holiness is finding and being our true selves, which are in the *image* of God. It is not presumption to be who you are; it is humility. When we are tenderhearted and forgiving, we are "imaging" God, acting as if we actually belonged to His family.

TRANSFORMATION

Forgiveness goes a long way, and when we accept it—really accept it as the incredible gift that it is—it is transformational. Valjean in Victor Hugo's *Les Misérables* is a bitter man who has been treated unfairly and cruelly for most of his life. He has spent 19 years in jail for stealing a loaf of bread and then later trying to escape his imprisonment. A little forgiveness earlier on would have made a huge difference in his life. Instead, the world has gotten far more than even with him: it has exacted the largest penalty and denied him the smallest chance. Yes, he felt that he had every right to even the score, and we would be hard-pressed to prove otherwise. What he did not anticipate was an act that would change his life.

Finding lodging one night at the home of a Catholic bishop, he is treated with great kindness and hospitality. But Valjean's soul is dead to such graces: all he can see is the opportunity to steal most of the household silver, which he does that night. As he attempts to flee with his loot, the police catch him. They bring him back to the bishop's house for identification. To their surprise, the bishop hands two silver candlesticks to Valjean and says, "You forgot these." Clearly, he is trying to give the police the impression that he had given Valjean the silver with which the man has now been caught. The police leave, and the bishop turns to his bewildered guest and says, "I have bought your soul for God." Years of bitterness dissolve, and Valjean becomes an entirely different man. The years ahead are tough, very tough, but the joy of them is immeasurable, and his own capacity for mercy seems to know no bounds. Forgiveness works like that.

Valjean is a one-man microcosm of the Church. The Church is a fellowship of saints transformed by forgiveness. They are transformed into forgiving people, and this is exactly what makes them an embarrassment to those who are otherwise inclined. They seem awkward because they don't march to the meter of a get-even world. They seem a bit dense because they don't jump at every opportunity to advantage themselves over others. They seem naive because they believe people can be radically changed. But if you see them against the background of a Kingdom that runs by grace, they are just about the right fit. Try to take advantage of one of them. They will probably forgive you, and then it would be much harder to play "get-even." You might even forgive someone yourself and suddenly find that you are not far from that Kingdom of the forgiving forgiven. And what are you going to do then? What *can* you do? Your soul has been bought for God.

Forgiveness is God's great outwitting of an unforgiving world. If anything completely fools the principalities and powers that hold the human race in bondage, it is the heaven-inspired unwillingness to get even. Such an unwillingness makes the rules inapplicable and completely redefines the game. If you want to outwit an adversary, forgive him. Do the opposite of what he expects, says the apostle Paul (Rom. 12:20-21). Satan's wiles might win the day, says Paul, but if you fight him with forgiveness of people, he is disarmed (2 Cor. 2:10-11).

Can you understand why forgiveness of our sins is such an important part of the liberating gospel message? Can you understand why forgiveness of others is probably the most empowering thing we can do for them? And can you understand why forgiven-forgiving people are the most joyful, and the holiest, on earth?

Go find a bunch of hilarious saints, and I guarantee you'll find people transformed by forgiveness.

9

Good Reason No. 2:
A Gracious Providence

The Church sees history as the story of God's providence. History is the story not only of humanity but also of God's involvement in the human story. In fact, it is God's story as much as it is ours.

Now Christians are very stubborn about this, about seeing God at work in history and in their own lives. But they don't see blindly, so to speak; they don't pretend that the signs and clues are always identifiable. In fact, they confess that God's face at times is hidden and the evidence hard to find.

There was a time, when He hung on the Cross, when even their Lord felt a divine abandonment (Mark 15:34; Matt. 27:46). The amazing thing is that Christians have come to understand that God was nowhere more present than on that Cross. They believe that here God poured out His life to save us. Before then, He had been deeply involved in the human story He had set in motion. But now, on the Cross, His story became our story, and ours became His, from then on.

Christians believe that if you want to get your own story straight, you have to check it out with God's story. The way to salvation is to let His story become your story, to allow His story to pull you in, claim you completely, and change your own narrative forever. The Church is a company of people who have been to this place where God's story became theirs and who have been living inside God's story ever since.

Living inside God's story is really the same as living in the kingdom of God that Jesus brought to us. This Kingdom is not so much a concept as it is the story of our rightful King at work, setting up a Kingdom unlike any other, inviting us every which way He can to enter it and enjoy it and creating a totally new, transforming story we can be a part of. The Church is a people with a new story.

And they're sticking to it. Even when things get tough or seemingly hopeless, Christians keep the story. The circumstances of the moment might suggest that their story isn't holding together very well, doesn't fit reality, is inadequate to the day. Or someone may invite the Christian to take a different story line, one that makes the person the central character of his or her own story, seemingly in charge of the outcome, master of his or her own universe. Or the Christian may be tempted to believe that there really is no story at all, only a steady stream of unpredictable, uncontrollable circumstances that he or she can only be resigned to and, at best, try to face bravely. But he or she sticks to God's story instead, realizing that it's the true reality, the main plot.

It's not that the believer places his or her faith in some divine blueprint. If there is a blueprint, we have only pieces of it. Life is fraught with unanswered questions, and much of history is unexplained, or perhaps unexplainable. What the believer places his or her faith in is the Author and main Character of the gospel story, and the ending.

The Church has traditionally referred to this trustworthy divine story line as *providence*. Born-again people believe that history in general and their own personal histories in particular are in the hands of a providential God. This knowledge gives them a deep joy that hard times and numerous detractors cannot steal from them. It also gives them the steadiness and purposefulness without which a life on track—a holy life—is impossible.

WALTER'S STORY

Perhaps the best way to talk about providence is to tell a true story.

It begins on a cold battlefield in France in 1918. An Englishman named Walter lay seriously wounded on the damp ground of a battle trench. For him, the end seemed very, very near, his story almost over. It had been five days now since that horrible onslaught that had wiped out all but two men from his platoon. Walter's body had taken a generous share of the bullets and shrapnel that had come their way that day.

Things were looking very bleak for Walter. The thread of life to which he had been clinging had become alarmingly thin. He felt the cold winds of death brushing his helpless body.

His life flashed before him. He remembered his happy, adventurous childhood years in a Midlands industrial town. He had been raised in a family who attended The Salvation Army. His love for God had been well nurtured. He wanted to serve God as a faithful "soldier" of that Ilkeston corps (congregation). Brass band music was his passion from childhood. He played his euphonium in the corps youth band, and when he reached the required age for membership in the senior band, he was given his longed-for place.

It wasn't long before another wonderful thing happened. A dark-haired, dark-eyed young woman in the corps named Miriam accepted his proposal for marriage, and they joined hand and heart for life. His job at the local steel plant gave them the security they needed. It was a good beginning to an adult life. Walter now had just about everything he wanted: a confident faith in God, marriage to the woman he loved, a supportive community of believers, an acceptable measure of economic security, and the prospect of a bright future.

But now his memories were being rudely interrupted by the sharp, stabbing pain of his wounds and by the chilling wind against which he had almost no protection. The British medic had ripped off his shirt to attempt brief treatment of the wounds before making his own hasty retreat in the face of the massive German onslaught. Now without a shirt, Walter had been exposed to the elements these five days. He knew he could not hold out much longer.

Almost in desperation, he began to recall the words of a song by an early Salvationist pioneer, John Lawley (it had become his favorite):

> *Though thunders roll and darkened be the sky,*
> *I'll trust in thee!*
> *Though joys may fade and prospects droop and die,*

I'll trust in thee!
No light may shine upon life's rugged way,
Sufficient is thy grace from day to day.

I'm not outside thy providential care,
I'll trust in thee!
I'll walk by faith thy chosen cross to bear,
I'll trust in thee!
Thy will and wish I know are for the best,
This gives to me abundant peace and rest.

Walter thought, "Where is His providence now? Am I really not outside His providential care?" He lay in the trench feeling very much alone in a world that seemed already to have forgotten him. Where was God?

Walter was eventually picked up by the German Red Cross, but this rescue from imminent death soon proved to be a terrible trial. The British blockade had worked so effectively that the Germans were left without adequate medical supplies, which, of course, were used primarily for their own wounded.

When it came time for the shrapnel to be removed from Walter's body, the surgeon's tools for Walter's already-infected wounds were rusty razor blades and paper bandages, along with limited quantities of antiseptic. It was impossible to get all the shrapnel, and the infection could not be stopped. There were several crude operations. Finally, he was pronounced incurable.

Eventually Walter was released to the Swiss Red Cross. He weighed 87 pounds. But in a hospital on the shores of Lake Constance, he was slowly nursed back to health.

Months later, his wife was sitting in the Sunday morning service at the Ilkeston Corps of The Salvation Army, trying to keep her 18-month-old child in tow. She heard shouts in the street. Walter had arrived unannounced. People on the streets had recognized him as he made his way from the railway station. Men were now carrying him on their shoulders as a spontaneous parade made its way to the corps building.

We can only imagine what went through Miriam's heart and mind when she saw her Walter. The British government had informed her that her husband was presumed dead. They had suggested that she apply for her war widow's pension. Reluctantly, she had. Now he stood before her. Miraculously, the family was reunited.

But the trials were not over for Walter. The wounds would not fully heal. He went through year after year of further surgery and treatment. About five and a half years later the family immigrated to the United States, where Walter and Miriam eventually became Salvation Army officers. But tragedy struck. Miriam became ill with cancer, suffered from it for years, and finally died at the young age of 45.

Walter eventually remarried, and he and his new wife, Mildred, served as officers until the damage that had been done to his body caught up with him and forced him to retire a few years early. Parkinson's disease and hardening of the arteries finally combined to throw him into physical disability and mental confusion. The best thing that could be said about his last years was that he endured them. He died hardly knowing anyone he loved.

If Walter could speak to us, what would he say about God's providential care? *He would say that God never left him, never forsook him.* He would also say that God had given him a joy that nothing could take away.

That's what my grandfather—Walter Dunmore Needham—would say. My most enduring memory of him is his laughter. Whenever we Needham children were told that Gramps and Auntie Mildred were coming for a visit, we knew that this unique man with fascinating bullet marks in his body would bring fun with him. I would hardly sleep the night before their arrival. Later, I lived with Gramps and Auntie Mildred (then retired) during my university years. I saw his deterioration rapidly progress. I saw his mind weaken and his emotions become confused. But I knew—and every now and then I would catch a glimpse of it in his eyes or his now faltering words—that the joy of the Lord was still there. When I remember Gramps, what I feel most of all is joy.

A FRAGILE LIFE

What I have come to appreciate is that our stories are very much like Walter's. His life was dealt blows that called providence into question. So are ours.

We all know what it means to be alone, abandoned, abused,

terribly misunderstood, frustrated beyond words, defeated, put at a serious disadvantage, or wounded in one way or another. We all know something of what Walter was feeling on that field of terrible loneliness. The Old Testament Jews knew as well. They came to understand that these desert experiences in their journey had reasons, though some of them never became clear in this life. First of all, bad things sometimes happened to the best of them, because providence was not an insurance policy against suffering. Job found that out. Providence was sometimes hidden, its outcome long-delayed. Second, difficult circumstances were sometimes a testing to strengthen faith, as well as character. And third, tragic circumstances were often the outcome of their own bumbling unfaithfulness: sin, the violation of our nature, had consequences.

Sometimes it was evident why bad things were happening; other times it was not. Should our suffering bring us to our knees in sincere repentance, or should we lift our heads in stubborn faith? It all depended. Who brought this on: we or God?

One thing is clear in Scripture: those who place their faith in God completely can trust the future. "The righteous shall be kept safe forever" (Ps. 37:28). The promise is for the "forever." Between now and then there are tough times, sometimes tragic times. People of providence learn how to await the outcome (vv. 7, 34).

STRENGTH THROUGH BROKENNESS

Walter believed in the providence of God, but it did not protect him from suffering and harm. God allowed horrible physical trials to come upon him. In fact, He has allowed the most hideous crimes to be committed against His very best: devout missionaries who became martyrs, courageous converts who paid the ultimate price for their conversion in a hostile homeland—the list is endless. And there was Jesus, of whom God seemed to ask more suffering than anyone has a right to ask of another.

What the suffering of Jesus found was that close to every Gethsemane is a ministering angel. God gets us through. Providence is not protection—it is provision. Jesus said to His disciples, "Do not fear those who kill the body but cannot kill the soul" (Matt. 10:28). And He went on to tell them that the Father who knew when a little sparrow fell to the ground—even knew the number of hairs on their own heads—knew all their circumstances (Matt. 10:29-31). He certainly knew their suffering, and He promised that He and the Father would get them through it. After all, He had "conquered the world" (John 16:33). The long run would prove it.

Why else would the apostle Paul have the nerve to say with such confidence, "We know that all things work together for good for those who love God, who are called according to his purpose" (Rom. 8:28)?

Work together for good? Yes, because temporal setbacks do not repeal eternal outcomes, and because setbacks can become stepping stones to maturity of spirit and depth of character. The apostle Peter says it this way: "In this you rejoice, even if now for a little while you have had to suffer various trials, so that the genuineness of your faith—being more precious than gold that, though perishable, is tested by fire—may be found to result in praise and glory and honor when Jesus Christ is revealed" (1 Pet. 1:6-7). God allows us to be broken, and at the broken places where He heals us, we become stronger.

THE LAST ENEMY

The final and most powerful threat to a providential journey is death. Like fragile glasses used often, we will inevitably break, and our mortal lives will be over. Most people work hard at diverting themselves from thoughts of death, while a few morbidly dwell on it nearly all the time. The people of providence, however, do neither: they accept death, and they know it can be an extremely difficult journey; but they also know, as Bonhoeffer said, that it is the last festival on the road to freedom. The apostle Paul speaks of dying with Christ every day (Gal. 2:19-20; 1 Cor. 15:31), preparing himself for the loss of all things so that he might gain Christ (Phil. 3:7-11). "For while we live," he says, "we are always being given up to death for Jesus' sake, so that the life of Jesus may be made visible in our mortal flesh. So death is at work in us" (2 Cor. 4:11-12).

There is a sense in which the people of God work at their deaths. They prepare themselves for what they will inevitably lose, and they "crucify" (put to death) what they have come to understand is a detriment, or even a serious threat, to their journey with God. Mortality is something they live with.

Life is fragile. The more we can stop pretending and hoping we can escape suffering, grieving, and the pain of death, the more we can get on with abundant living. A God trusted will take the cruel misfortunes that threaten to shatter us, and in His own inscrutable way He will bring blessing and purpose. "You meant to do me harm," said Joseph to his brothers, who had maliciously sold him into slavery in a foreign land, "but God meant to bring good out of it by preserving the lives of many people, as we see today" (Gen. 50:20, NEB). Joseph had endured one life-threatening trial after another, his life only a quick blow away from obliteration. But he found a God who could be trusted.

INSCRUTABLE GENEROSITY

The people of providence know more than how fragile life is. They know *a God who is exceedingly gracious*.

During those terrible days when death seemed almost certain, Walter thought not only about all he would now probably be losing. He also must have asked, "Why me? Have I not lived a good life—not perfect, I'll grant you—but certainly a better-than-average life? Have I not served my Lord faithfully? What's the reason I'm being subjected to this? Am I paying the consequences for a few things left undone that I ought to have done?"

Providence is not a reward for being good—it is God's inscrutable generosity. All of us are here today because of one undeserved good turn after another. Ezekiel uses the shocking imagery of a newborn infant rejected and cast out into an open field, still covered with blood, unwashed, naked, unprotected, with its umbilical cord still uncut. The doomed infant is Judah, who has nothing for which to be commended. God passes by in that field of death, sees the dying infant, and says, "Live!" (Ezek. 16:6). He takes the baby and makes this little castoff someone special, a treasure coveted and loved. Here is Ezekiel's description of the transformation: "You grew exceedingly beautiful, fit to be a queen. Your fame spread among the nations on account of your beauty, for it was perfect because of my splendor that I had bestowed on you, says the Lord GOD" (16:13-14).

God claims a fragile someone with no commendation and makes that someone the special object of His care. This is providence.

In fact, sometimes God is good to people like us even when we're bad. He certainly was not attracted to Jacob because of the man's goodness. Jacob was a crafty, manipulative scoundrel. But Scripture says this: "He [God] sustained him [Jacob] in a desert land, in a howling wilderness waste; he shielded him, cared for him, guarded him as the apple of his eye" (Deut. 32:10).

TRUSTING OBEDIENCE

Does this mean, then, that we can presume upon that generosity? Should we abandon any attempt at goodness because providence is the undeserved gift of God, not the calculated outcome of good behavior? Does God see us through no matter how faithful we are (or aren't) to Him?

Of course not. Though providence is not deserved, it is certainly not a cheap giveaway. It is God's abiding presence with those who open their hearts to Him—as even Jacob finally did—and seek to live in obedience to Him. The Scriptures do not teach, "Be good and you'll be rewarded" but rather "Be obedient and God will open up the future to you." As we read in Ps. 84:11, "No good thing does the LORD withhold from those who walk uprightly."

How does this obedience come? By trying hard? Not really. It comes when we trust God enough to step out in faith. God is generous, not that we may try Him, but that we may trust Him. Trust Him to care for us and see us through. But also trust Him to guide us into obedience. At the dedication of the new Temple in Jerusalem, King Solomon expresses deep gratitude to God for His amazing providential care over the people of Israel. Then he prays for His continued presence with them. At this point he asks for something very specific—he asks that God will "incline our hearts to him, to walk in all his ways, and to keep his commandments, his statutes, and his ordinances, which he commanded our ancestors" (1 Kings 8:58).

The obedient are not the ones who grit their teeth and grimly carry out religious duties. They are the ones who relax and allow God to incline their hearts to Him, which He is more than pleased to do for all who hunger and thirst after righteousness.

A GOD TRUE TO HIS WORD

The people of providence also know that amid the cacophonies of contradictions and objections, God's truth abides. "The grass withers, the flower fades; but the word of our God will stand forever" (Isa. 40:8).

When everything seems to be caving in, we can stake our lives on God and that fact that He is always true to His Word. John Bunyan was imprisoned for his faith and faced a possible death sentence. He was afraid to die, but he wrote this: "I am for going on, and venturing my eternal state with Christ, whether I have comfort here or no. If God doth not come in, thought I, I will leap off the Ladder even blindfolded into Eternity, sink or swim, come Heaven, come Hell. Lord Jesus, if thou wilt catch me, do; if not, I will venture for thy Name."

A Future to Be Trusted

Providence is trusting the Provider.

On this side of eternity, God does not guarantee solutions to everything. However, He does guarantee that He will sustain us as He leads us to the future His Word has promised. How we come to that future is not always clear, but the future itself is. The future is where God's promises become reality. The people of promise are sure of this: *the future is exceedingly trustworthy.*

During those terrible days on the battlefield, Walter thought about the future that might have been. He had his dreams. He didn't have to go to war—he had not been drafted into the British army since he worked in a war-priority industry. But he wanted to do his part in the war that many believed would be "the war to end all wars." He was on that battlefield to build a future.

Walter had no idea what that future would look like. He only knew then that now he might well not live to see it. Since leaving on this last tour of duty, his wife, Miriam, had delivered their first and only child. It looked as if he might never lay eyes on his only son. His future on earth was a big question mark.

There was only one thing he knew for sure, and it was decisive: his future belonged to God, and God would see him through to it. God had promised, and His word could be trusted.

> *That word above all earthly pow'rs,*
> *No thanks to them, abideth;*
> *The Spirit and the gifts are ours*
> *Thro' Him who with us sideth.*

Let goods and kindred go—
This mortal life also.
The body they may kill;
God's truth abideth still.
His kingdom is forever.
—Martin Luther

The crucial battle had taken place many years before on a Cross. There a victory had been won for all time. The mortal flesh of a man named Walter might perish on this battlefield in France, but all of history was moving toward completion of the already-won war. Walter could perish—and still win. Providence is not a premature solution; it is the promise of eternity.

WAITING

We live in a society of spoiled children. People want immediate returns, instantaneous information, fast foods, overnight fortunes, painless cures, and quick fixes. The world is gratifying itself to death. It seems that the only way the modern mind can grasp providence is to make it into something God does for us right away, and in recent years an ample supply of "God give it to me now" hucksters have appeared on the church scene to appeal to that incessant craving for gratification.

But providence is not God spoiling us every day; it is the promise of eternity. The children of His providence know how to wait, and the truly wonderful things in life happen to those who are willing to live by God's timing and trust His future.

To be sure, there are times of deep fulfillment: moments when everything seems to come together perfectly, emotional peaks, times when "the joy that no one can take away" is in full bloom. These are previews, "foretastes of glory divine," and we treasure these moments and the memory of them. They are intimations of our future in Christ.

But that future is not spelled out for us in detail. It is a future that God will bring to pass in His own way. Providence is the trustworthiness of a gracious Person. No matter what the immediate circumstances seem to be saying about their future prospects, the people of providence will not let go of the One who says, "You're not outside My providential care."

JOY NO MATTER WHAT

What is providence? If you had asked my grandfather, he would have told you that it's not about wonderful careers, care-free living, and comfortable retirements. It's about a God who will never leave us or forsake us. It's about a God who has given us eternity.

Walter's story helps me see the guiding hand of God in my own. But most of all, it helps me see the smiling face of God in it. I think of times when hilarity broke through his normally shy demeanor. I now know it was a touch of God, a transcendence that sustained him through sometimes horrible circumstances and now made joy possible. The fact that Gramps could laugh was a miracle.

Providence is the unfailing hand of the Writer of the lead story that defines history and transforms our own stories. It gives laughter to those who need lifting above the bitter drafts of their circumstances. It makes glad sense of holy living in a world that otherwise would be able to offer no strong rationale for righteousness. History is moving toward the fulfillment of God's purposes in Christ, and holiness is the joyful journey of those who have become so hooked by this compelling story that they have made it their own. The song they sing as they journey is this: "Our steps are made firm by the LORD, when he delights in our way; though we stumble, we shall not fall headlong, for the LORD holds us by the hand" (Ps. 37:23-24).

10

※

Good Reason No. 3: A Delightful Presence

When you think about it, it only makes sense that hilarity infects the Church. After all, God is there.

Now, of course, God is everywhere. It's His nature to be. He can't help it. There's only one exception to this: hell. Whatever we know about hell, this is what makes hell unique—it's where God is not. All of us have had "hellish" experiences when a loving God seemed to be absent, though we later may have realized that He was not. The Christian faith also teaches that since love without freedom is meaningless, God actually gives persons a choice about living in His presence. If they want, they can choose to live as if He didn't exist. That's a type of hell on earth.

The Church is a community that has chosen otherwise, chosen to live in God's presence and enjoy Him forever. Actually, though, it started the other way around. In Christ, God chose to be with us (John 15:16), and we chose to be chosen—or to put it more accurately, we chose the Chooser. For us, the whole point of the Kingdom banquet feast is the presence of the Host. Our God loves to be with His people, and we to be with Him. This is why the Incarnation is at the very heart of the gospel. It tells us that God really does want to be with us and that He has taken all the necessary steps to do so. He made His presence known: first as a crying, demanding baby, then as a piercing, prophetic voice and as an acclaimed healer, then as a scandalous sacrifice, and finally as One who ever since has been everywhere through His Spirit, popping up in unexpected places and inviting us into His fellowship. It all began 2,000 years ago with this launching called the Incarnation "when the goodness and loving kindness of God our Savior appeared" (Titus 3:4). And it hasn't stopped since.

God's Friendship

One might well ask why God would act like this, why He would choose to spend so much time with us. He has His reasons, of course, and theologians have a heyday trying to explain them all. But one of His reasons is very apparent—and surprising, if not downright embarrassing, in the world of religion. Many religions see "God" as an ideal representing the perfection toward which we aspire or into which we hope eventually to be absorbed. Others see Him as an impersonal creator who sets everything in motion and sits back to watch with chilling detachment. Some see Him as a demanding judge who must be appeased again and again. Still others see Him as an indulgent father figure with no backbone or real engagement with us. But true Christians say one thing about God that is quite unusual: they say *God is a Friend*. This is why He wants to spend time with us.

We get a glimpse of this even in the Old Testament. Isaiah hears God calling Abraham "my friend" (41:8) and Israel "my beloved" (5:1) and "my delight" (62:4). We're told that Moses regularly spent time with God in the tent of meeting and that there "the Lord used to speak to Moses face to face, as one speaks to a friend" (Exod. 33:11). Jeremiah laments that because of Judah's sin, God has had to give "the beloved of my heart into the hands of her enemies" (Jer. 12:7). Then there's the Song of Solomon. While we're rightly cautioned against sublimating its honest, life-affirming poetry of sexual love and against forcing allegorical interpretations that are not clearly indicated or even intimated, it's certainly no accident that over the centuries Jewish and Christian interpreters have drawn the parallels to the intimate love between God and His people: God, it seems, wants to be on very familiar terms with us. It seems that He also sticks by us and does not give up on us even when we abandon Him and seek the lesser intimacies that degrade us. Hosea tells us all about that (chap. 2).

The New Testament not only picks up this message but brings it right home. God the Friend becomes a friend-in-the-flesh. Friendship with God becomes as palpable as a relationship with Jesus and all Jesus' friends. Jesus says to His disciples that they are much more than His students and His servants, though they are indeed these. He says, "I have called you friends" (John 15:15). It's no accident that the time He spends with people is not all preaching and healing. He also spends time with them at parties and dinners, as well as in private conversation. That's what friends do. When He tells the parable of the great dinner, He's talking about a friendship banquet, and the refusal of some invited guests to attend is clearly a rejection of God's friendship (Luke 14:15-24). God wants to be our Friend, and I dare say there's the longing somewhere in us all to have a God who loves us and enjoys us in a friendlike way.

But when it comes to God, we're not used to that way of thinking. We may think it only right to keep a respectful distance—after all, we're talking about the God of the universe! Overfamiliarity with the divine can be blasphemous and presumptuous. Some think they treat God with respect by pushing Him away and making Him less accessible.

In the meantime, God is saying, "Let Me take care of My own transcendence. I'll manage to be God no matter what you do or don't do. What I need help with is being your Friend. That takes both of us. Oh, I can be a Friend to you no matter what you do, but what makes Me glad is for you to *accept* Me as your Friend."

Companion on the Journey

In the final analysis, a relationship with God doesn't mean much unless you like His company. His presence is what makes the real difference. "Where thou art," prayed Thomas à Kempis, "there is heaven; and where thou art not, behold, there is death and hell." Friendship with God is the doorway to joy. A king of Judah is made "glad with the joy of [God's] presence" (Ps. 21:6), and one particular king reveals his longing for that presence in this way: "One thing I asked of the LORD, that will I seek after: to live in the house of the LORD all the days of my life, to behold the beauty of the LORD, and to inquire in his temple" (27:4). Nothing could delight him more than God's presence.

It's the poor, however, who especially delight in God's friendship. They cry out in their troubles, and like a good friend, God hears and acts (34:6). He stands by them and defends them (109:31). When He appears in human form, He spends most of His time with them, preaching to them (Luke 4:18), inviting them to His symbolic banquet (14:13), sharing their lives, and giving them the joy of His company (John 3:29). No one who is excluded from association with others because of social status or powerlessness is excluded from this company. Jesus is Friend to all.

Every friendship, of course, has a history. Friends are those we travel through life with in significant ways; they help us to define our journey, set our course and stay on it; they are there when we need them to understand us and love us. After all, what are friends for? And where would we be without them?

God is a Friend like that, and more than that. He loves us as we are, and also as what He knows we are becoming. He travels alongside us, and also before us. He helps us understand the way, and also shows us the way. The fact is that we are lost without Him. That's why Christians are those who have chosen to travel this earth with God. For them, God is *a Companion on the journey*.

BROKEN FRIENDSHIP

Very tenderly the prophet Hosea speaks of God's companionship with His people, those who have chosen to journey with Him. Unfortunately, His people have become rebellious and have left the journey to pursue other companionships, relationships that lead nowhere, friendships that prove to be a deception. God's lament is a remembrance of their journey together, a recital of His intimate, loving leadership of them: "It was I who taught Ephraim to walk, I took them up in my arms; but they did not know that I healed them. I led them with cords of human kindness, with bands of love. I was to them like those who lift infants to their cheeks. I bent down to them and fed them" (11:3-4).

Why would we turn our backs on this shepherding God? You tell *me*. I don't know why we choose the lesser when the best is so available. I simply can't comprehend our chasing after gods that deceive and degrade us. It obviously has something to do with wanting to be on our own, as if *anyone* was truly on his or her own. We, all of us, travel with companions. That's how we're made: to be with others. Even the recluse lives his or her life with others, even if those persons are conjured up only in memory or imagination. Being "on our own" is a fiction akin to Satan's lie told in the garden: we can be totally self-sufficient, like gods, able to decide entirely for ourselves what's good for us and what's not (Gen. 3:1-5). I don't understand why it is that we buy this fiction, why we fool ourselves that we can travel alone when all we can actually do is choose far lesser companions for the journey.

JOURNEY WITH GOD

God invites us to journey with Him. He does not call from afar and say, "Try to reach Me." He says, "Let's travel together."

The understanding of life as a journey with God is a powerful metaphor in Scripture. For 40 years the people of Israel journeyed to Canaan. It should not have taken that long, even by foot. But it did because they kept getting jittery when things got tough, and they started doubting that God was traveling with them, or if He was, that He was the kind of companion they wanted to travel with. Moses had convinced them that God was leading them out of Egypt to some Promised Land, but they were not long off the starting line before the first challenge came, and they jumped all over Moses for telling them that this was all God's idea and that He would see them through (Exod. 14:11-12). God met the challenge spectacularly by parting the waters for their escape. But soon afterward the food supply ran low, and they complained again. This time God rained bread from heaven (chap. 16). Then it was Rephidim, where they ran out of water. By now they were ready to stone Moses, but God told him to strike the rock with his staff and water would come out. It did, and once again God proved His presence. Moses named the place Meribah ("Quarrel"), because "the Israelites quarreled and tested the LORD, saying, 'Is the LORD among us or not?'" (17:1-7). That was indeed the question: Was He?

Once the Israelites settled in Canaan, their spiritual leaders and prophets told them to remember those journey days when God traveled with them as their companion Lord, communed with them on the journey, and saw them through to the end. The threat to faith now was to reduce it to prescribed rituals that were supposed to guarantee the Companion's blessing and favor regardless of the people's conduct. The luring temptation was to abandon the journey with God and substitute a settled religiosity that called on God only when needed. Over time most of them forgot their Companion on the journey. "Is the Lord among us or not?"

One prophet after another told them that He was not. It was bad enough that the people were sinning against Him and one another. It was even worse that they were living on their own, without Him. Oh, they did expect Him to hang around at a distance and come quickly when called upon to get them out of a fix or avert a national disaster; otherwise, they wished He would stay away. Jeremiah describes God's view of this state of affairs: "My people have committed two evils: they have forsaken me, the fountain of living water, and dug out cisterns for themselves, cracked cisterns that can hold no water" (Jer. 2:13).

The way to ensure God's absence is to forsake Him. The way to keep Him close is to practice His presence and His lifestyle, to "do justice, and to love kindness, and to walk humbly with your God" (Mic. 6:8).

A FRIEND FOREVER

This is where Jesus enters the picture, the God we can humbly walk with, a God-in-the-flesh Companion. The Word became flesh and dwelt among us. Then He walked among us and with us. Then He died among us and for us. Then He was raised, the first among us and for us. Then as the Holy Spirit He came among us forever. The whole scenario screams the news that God cares more deeply for us than we can imagine and longs for the delight of our companionship.

Companionship: that's what He really wants. Caring for us: that's what He really wants to do. Jesus once referred to himself as "the good shepherd" (John 10:11). The hired hand, He said, does not finally care for the sheep; his interest in them is defined only by the pay he gets for tending them. But the good shepherd genuinely cares for the sheep; he knows them, and they know him. Jesus went even further than the analogy would logically allow: the good shepherd gives his life for the sheep. It was the supreme act of a true companion and friend, one which, in this case, made Him a Friend forever.

A Christian is someone who has a Friend forever. His or her true home is not a place; it is *an abiding in Christ.* Jesus draws upon yet another image of intimacy: He says He is the vine and we are its branches. He instills our very nature, forms our character, serves as our life source, provides all the security we need, and creates the bond of a relationship that defines and values us. Here is how He put it:

> I am the vine. You are the branches. Those who abide in me and I in them bear much fruit, because apart from me you can do nothing. . . . If you abide in me, and my words abide in you, ask for whatever you wish, and it will be done for you. My Father is glorified by this, that you bear much fruit and become my disciples. As the Father has loved me, so I have loved you; abide in my love. . . . I have said these things to you so that my joy may be in you, and that your joy may be complete *(John 15:5, 7-9, 11).*

ABIDING IN CHRIST

Joy is abiding in Christ, who is God abiding with us. The Old Testament writers knew that God's presence could sometimes be a fearful thing, especially when His people had abandoned Him for lesser gods: His delight in them was nothing to be taken for granted. While followers of other cults made sacrifices of appeasement to displeased gods, seeking to curry favor (not to draw near), the best spiritual leaders of Israel saw the sacrifices for sin as the opening of a door to God, the restoration of a relationship. In the ceremony of covenant ratification, after the offerings of well-being had been made and the book of the covenant read and affirmed, Moses, Aaron, Nadab, Abihu, and the 70 elders "went up, and they saw the God of Israel. . . . They beheld God" (Exod. 24:9-11). The real joy came with the restored Presence, not with the temporary reprieve. The real joy was communing with God. Thus Moses' greatness lay not so much in his flawed accomplishments, impressive as they were, as in his being the one "whom the LORD knew face to face" (Deut. 34:10). Thus David's heart prayer: "Do not hide your face from me" (Ps. 27:9). Thus another psalmist's cry: "When shall I come and behold the face of God?" (42:2).

"Look to him," says David, "and be radiant" (34:5). If joy

was to be found, it would be found in seeing God and abiding in His company.

In the New Testament this desire for God finds its fulfillment through the coming of Christ in Jesus of Nazareth. Quoting Isaiah, the evangelist Matthew says that this Messiah's name is "Emmanuel," which means "God is with us" (1:23). The whole life and ministry of Jesus can be seen in terms of that name: everything He is and does reveals how God is now present with us in this radically new way—this available, immediate, human way. The Word is now flesh, dwelling among us, exposing the very glory of God (John 1:14). God is as close, or closer, as the neighbor next door.

Unseparating Death

No wonder Jesus' disciples become so dismayed when He finally tells them that He's going away (though He's been with them only three short years). What happened to "God is with us"? How can God raise our expectations like this and then suddenly, cruelly, leave us in the cold of a sudden retreat? Why is Jesus abandoning us now?

The answer, of course, is that death has now lost its separating power. For those who long for God, for those who now follow Christ through the valley of the shadow of a conquered death, death itself is a doorway into the eternal Presence. The early disciples don't grasp it immediately—they think they've lost their Savior, and with Him their future. But things soon start happening that cause them to recall something He had said to them: "So you have pain now; but I will see you again, and your hearts will rejoice, and no one will take your joy from you" (John 16:22).

A few days after Jesus' death, the disciples are huddled in fear behind closed doors. They suddenly see something that stretches their credulity and lifts their spirits at the same time: a resurrected Jesus. He says to them, "Peace be with you" (John 20:19). As if to establish identity, He shows them the nail marks on His hands and the spear mark on His side. And they rejoice.

The same day two other disciples are on their way to Emmaus, puzzling through the events of the last few days, especially the empty tomb. Unrecognized, the resurrected Lord draws near and joins them on the journey. He begins to make sense out of all this confusion. Intrigued, they prevail upon Him to join them for supper. And there, in the communion of that meal, in the sharing of their deepest concerns, in the opening of the Scriptures, their eyes are opened. They recognize Him. They recognize the presence of God: "Were not our hearts burning within us?" (Luke 24:32).

The good news is that death does not rob us of His presence—it ushers us into it. It brings a gift: the eternal delight of God's company. In the parable of the talents, those who have been faithful and fruitful in what has been entrusted to them receive the invitation for which they've longed: "Enter into the joy of your master" (Matt. 25:21, 23).

This is joy: abiding in His presence now as well as forever. The Church is that group for whom God is now a close Neighbor, an intimate Friend, a trustworthy Presence. The apostle Paul speaks in the vibrant present when he says to the Philippian congregation, "The Lord is near. Do not worry about anything, but in everything by prayer and supplication with thanksgiving let your requests be made known to God. And the peace of God, which surpasses all understanding, will guard your hearts and your minds in Christ Jesus" (Phil. 4:5-7).

SEEING US THROUGH

If the Church believes its own message, it has nothing to fear. The Lord is near—always. He is not an insulation against tough times or intense suffering, but always there, always sufficient, and in one way or another seeing us through.

I recently heard Margaret White, a retired Salvation Army officer, recount a story told by Kebokile Dengu from then Rhodesia when she was training for officership at the International Training College in London. It is set in 1979 when there was much confusion in war-torn Rhodesia. Rebel soldiers were roaming the countryside; some of them were killing indiscriminately.

Kebokile had an officer-friend whose husband had to leave her alone one weekend. As the evening darkness .settled, she grew afraid. A loud hammering at the door completely unsettled her. In her terror she prayed, "Lord, there's only me and the cat. Stand by me!"

At the door she found four youths, armed with guns and obviously trigger-happy. Again she prayed her desperate silent prayer, "Lord, stand by me!" The youths simply looked at her. Finally one of them said, "Good evening," and they left.

Later in the week she met one of the young men in the marketplace. He said to her, "We had come to kill you that night. Who was the man standing beside you?"

That night the Lord was a protective shield. Sometimes in those situations He is not, but rather the good, strong Shepherd who lovingly leads us through the valley of the shadow of death, the Friend who helps us realize that death need not be feared because it cannot separate the two of us, nor ultimately all of us who walk it with Him.

Heaven Now

Heaven is being with God. It is the unending enjoyment of His company and dancing to His delight. Some Christians think they have to wait for heaven. The art of Christian living is the art of living in heaven now, practicing the presence of God even—and especially—when we are most tempted to miss or dismiss Him.

Christians are those who have been called to see and expose and praise God just about everywhere, just about all the time. A monk in an ancient Celtic monastery even wrote, "and when I sleep, my snores are songs of praise." Every Christian worth his or her salt knows that God is always close enough to touch. He is everywhere.

How, then, do we help people to see Him, people who have plenty of evidence to deny His existence, or at least His interest in us, and whose vision has been trained to discern anything but the presence and work of God in the world and in their lives? There is more than one way. But I think that the best way was hinted at (oddly enough) in Steven Spielberg's movie *Close Encounters of the Third Kind*. This movie portrays a creature more wonderful than man. But we never see the creature itself. We only see wonder and awe in the eyes of those who gaze upon it. We only see an undeniable reflection in the faces of those who see.

Christians are people dazzled by the reflections of God in their world, who themselves become dazzling with their own reflections of Him. I am not using "dazzling" here to describe a brilliant performance, an impressive feat, or a really good show. I am using it to mean something that stuns or stupefies, a light that brings an image that gives us a start and unsettles us with a new presence. We don't need to be impressive to be dazzling. We need only abide in Christ and genuinely live our lives within the reality of His companionship. We will then shock some people who look at us expecting to find one thing and instead find Christ. They find the joy of those who have the privilege of Jesus' company and the influence of His character. They find people becoming holy as they companion with Jesus and become more like Him. They find people "with unveiled faces, seeing the glory of the Lord as though reflected in a mirror . . . being transformed into the same image from one degree of glory to another" (2 Cor. 3:18).

You can see why this holiness is often uncontainable. You can see why it breaks the molds of self-interested conduct and artificial happiness. You can see why it's the true freedom, the freedom of those who relax in Jesus' presence and find their humanity in His reflection. The people of God are those who have discovered who they are through a Friend. They surprise themselves every day with who they're becoming with Him. The change is so unpredictable and miraculous, it's hilarious.

That may be why the true Church laughs so much.

11

Good Reason No. 4: Encouragement from Others

In one of A. A. Milne's stories, Pooh Bear is about to go for a walk in the Hundred Acre Wood. It's about 11:30 in the morning—yes, a fine time to go calling—just before lunch. Pooh sets out across the stream, stepping on the stones, and when he gets to the middle of the stream, he sits down on a warm stone and thinks about just where would be the best place to make a call. He says to himself, "I think I'll go see Tigger." No, he dismisses that. Then he says, "Owl!" Then "No, Owl uses big words, hard-to-understand words." At last he brightens up. "I know! I think I'll go see Rabbit. I like Rabbit. Rabbit uses encouraging words like 'How's about lunch?' and 'Help yourself, Pooh!' Yes, I think I'll go see Rabbit."

During the years when Keitha and I read children's stories with our daughters, we became acutely aware that the material often dealt with some of the simplest but deepest human needs. It doesn't take a trained psychotherapist to figure out what Pooh needs as he sits on that warm rock in the middle of the stream, puzzling over which friend to go see: he needs encouragement. And however self-sufficient and tightly wrapped we may think we are, so do we. Without it, our confidence shrivels, and we diminish ourselves—or, far worse, we turn our rejection on others.

We may not need encouragement for our survival. In fact, if mere survival is the issue, we can probably exist without encouragement. But if we're speaking of something far more important, if we're speaking of becoming who we really are in God's image, then encouragement is crucial. Encouragement helps keep the soul on its journey with God. It's someone seeing the grace of God at work in another person's life, affirming that person to the core and encouraging him or her to claim the future God has in store.

The word "encouragement" has been used in different ways, and some of them have little or nothing to do with what I'm talking about. Cheering someone up is sometimes helpful, but I'm referring to something more substantive. Pep talks are often disguised manipulation. Giving hope without foundation is a setup for disillusionment. Attempting to eliminate all forms of discouragement in someone's life is paternalism. And endlessly indulging someone because we don't want to discourage the person is to weaken him or her.

True encouragement is something quite different from all these shallower imitations. It's something much truer, something that builds spiritual strength and brings lasting joy. As the word itself implies, it means giving someone courage, strengthening confidence. This is the kind of solid affirmation that comes from those who care about us deeply and stand by us firmly. Encouragement is love in action when confidence is lagging. It is from Philemon's love that the apostle Paul has received "much joy and encouragement" (v. 7). Joy indeed. Few things bring more joy than someone we care about believing in us when we find it difficult to believe in ourselves.

Vivid images often help us grasp the meaning of something. I want to share three images that for me convey the life-changing power of encouragement.

YOUR CHEERLEADERS ON THE SIDELINES

Picture yourself on a sports field of some kind. The game is your life. For you, encouragement is *someone standing along the sidelines and cheering you on.*

Who are *your* cheerleaders? For me, they are Mom and Dad; teachers who took an interest; my pastors and spiritual mentors who took the time and went to the trouble to nurture me in the faith, sharing the fruit of their thinking and the passion of their heart; caring colleagues who challenged and tested me; friends for life whose affirmation of me means more than they could ever know; and above all, my wife, Keitha, my favorite cheerleader, who has given me courage for as long as I've known her and will continue to do so till death us do part. When I'm in the heat of battle and look over to the sidelines for help, I look for these people and others like them. I look for those in whose faces I see the face of a cheering God. I look for my encouragers.

Jackie Joyner Kersee's encourager was the grandmother who named and raised her. She named her after Jackie Kennedy, "because someday she's going to be the first lady of something!" The prophecy was given, the blessing was bestowed, and Joyner grew up in an atmosphere of promise with a cheerleading grandmother on the sidelines, believing in her. Forget the birth defect—this child of the promise became the first lady of track and field.[1]

I've mentioned my own parents as two of my most important encouragers. From my mother the encouragement seemed to flow as easily and naturally as the Mississippi and was almost as massive. She surely must have uttered a discouraging word or two somewhere along the way, but I can't remember one. What I do remember is that she was always there on the sidelines, shouting quietly her believing words.

My father's encouragement was more complicated. He was a strong authority figure, and we often tangled, sometimes to a standoff. Some of our competitiveness stemmed from our personality differences, some from a need to find my own ground to stand on, and some, I must admit, from my sheer rebelliousness. But in ways that still amaze me, this formidable father of mine was often able to enjoy me and make it easy for me to enjoy him. He found common ground.

When the family lived in Charlotte, North Carolina, with my older brother away at college and my two other siblings still too young for "outdoor evangelism," it was my father and I who drove downtown to participate in our church's "open-air meeting." To be perfectly honest, this was not high on my list of favorite activities, though I knew we were helpful to some of the people on the streets we contacted during and after those meetings. But there was something else my father and I shared: a passion for the Saturday evening *Perry Mason* television series about the brilliant lawyer who always won his case and vindicated the innocent. When our evangelistic work downtown had drawn to a conclusion, we both looked at our watches for a quick calculation of how many minutes we had before the program started. Saturday night traffic was mercifully light, and we always made it home in very good time. We never missed a program. "We"—it was a shared passion, a secret, carefully timed routine that belonged only to us, one of the little things my father fashioned, probably unconsciously, to find common ground between us.

During my high school years, I came to believe that my father also enjoyed tropical fish as a hobby. I had developed a keen interest in it, and at one time my bedroom had up to 15 aquariums. The scaly creatures prospered under my diligent care, and my fellow enthusiast and right-hand helper was my father.

The real test of our commitment, however, was the dirty work: cleaning the aquariums. It was not pleasant. Stubborn algae had to be scrubbed off the sides, but far worse than that was the cleaning of the sand. It had become the repository of biological waste and decayed vegetation, exuding an aroma sufficient to send any sensitive soul running. Only those who loved this hobby, truly loved it, could survive the ordeal. And we did, my father and I. I loved it so much that I chose to attend one of the few universities that had a school of marine biology.

The most interesting thing of all is that once I had left home and gone off to college, my father permanently ceased his involvement with this hobby. He was no longer interested. It became clear to me later what his seemingly keen interest in tropical fish had been all about. He had seen my own interest in it and had decided to use it to get next to me and encourage me. It was a way to connect—on my turf and on my terms. He entered my playing field and became my cheerleader. As I reflect back on those days and let myself feel what those hours together with my father were like, I honor them as a way of affirming who I was. It was his gift to me. I did not become a marine biologist, but underwater life still holds great fascination for me, and I always enjoy studying aquariums. I just don't want to clean them anymore.

I imagine most of us have memories that encourage us, memories of key characters in our stories who have stood cheering on the sidelines and still do, if only in our memories.

Christians have a wonderful Book of encouraging memories. In fact, one thing you could say about Christians is that they are people who adopt this Book wholesale and make its memories their own. They are forever remembering what the Bible remembers. They remember God's dealings with the children of Israel and how He never, never let them down. They remember the coming of Jesus, God's fullness and faithfulness in the flesh, remember this most important pivotal event in history. They remember the Old Testament heroes of the faith who died without having yet received what was promised but had seen and greeted it from afar. They remember the New Testament heroes of the faith who lived to see the promise fulfilled and staked their lives on its reality. Christians remember with the Bible, and the memories encourage them in their pilgrimage.

They also remember their own special "cloud of witnesses." Baptist preacher and writer Carlyle Marney called them his "balcony people." These were the people he looked up to, those from whom he received affirmation and drew strength, the ones with lives worth emulating. They brought out the best in him; they were his encouragement.

Who are your encouragers? Who are the people on your sidelines, applauding you on to your own particular greatness? Name them. Thank God for them. And move on ahead to the sound of their cheers. They're God's gifts to you. They're your "church," your cloud of witnesses, your own loyal company of cheerleaders.

YOUR COMPANIONS ON THE JOURNEY

Another image that for me conveys the life-changing power of encouragement is *a companion on the journey*. Our best encouragers do more than cheer us on. When we need them, they travel alongside us, and they stand by our side through thick and thin.

You probably know that the reason Canada geese fly in a V-shape is so that the updraft from the lead goose can make it easier for those behind him to fly with less expenditure of energy. The geese alternate with that lead spot because it is more demanding than the others. What is it that keeps the occupant of that strenuous position going? Many believe that it's the reassuring honks from the other geese. The one who needs the encouragement is the one who gets it.

I was even more intrigued to learn what happens when one

of the geese is injured, perhaps by pellets from a hunter's gun, and has to fall out of formation to the ground. Usually two other geese also fall out of formation and stay on the ground with their companion until either he dies from his wounds or he heals sufficiently to continue the journey. The one who needs a brother or sister by his side is the one who gets it. Now where did this otherwise very aggressive species get the idea that none of them should suffer alone? With their dominating nature and their facility at propagation, I doubt that this particular action is a crucial built-in strategy for the survival of the species. Of course, it's stretching the imagination too far to suggest that, whatever else He is up to here, the Creator is trying to teach us what He is like, and what we can be like, as well. Or is it?

We all need companionship on the journey, especially in the tough times. The Church at its best abounds with those kinds of encouragers, those who will leave the sidelines and become our on-site support system. The apostle Paul knew this well. He instructed the Galatian Christians to "bear one another's burdens" (6:2). He urged the Thessalonians to "encourage one another and build up each other" (1 Thess. 5:11). The Ephesian church was told that each member had received a ministry gift to equip the saints for the work of ministry so that the Body of Christ could be "built up." (The Greek word here, *oikodomeo*, literally meant building or erecting a structure, but it had also come to mean encouraging, edifying, or strengthening someone. Encouragement helps people build their lives.) The object of the "building up" is for the Body of Christ to "come to the unity of the faith and of the knowledge of the Son of God, to maturity, to the measure of the full stature of Christ" (Eph. 4:12-13). Christians come alongside one another, share their concern and the ministry for which they have been gifted, and by doing so encourage each other into their future in Christ.

God is in the business of sending us helpers. Sometimes they're encouraging companions on the journey, as Barnabas was to Paul. Sometimes they're rescuers who find us in our desperation and help us come through, as Jonathan did for David. All of us need them, and without them we are left with the sadness of a lonely isolation.

Your Mentors at the Door

The third image of encouragement is *a mentor at the door*.

Not only do we need those who will cheer us on and those who will share our journey and be there when we need them, but also we need those who will open doors for us, those who believe in us, walk us through the room of our fears and self-doubts, and show us a door to new possibilities.

Door openers are like Moses, who late in his life stood on the brink of the Promised Land knowing that he would not be crossing over. The Lord had told him to encourage Joshua, his successor, and to be his door opener (Deut. 1:38; 3:28). That's precisely what he did (31:7-8; 34:9). And Joshua walked through the door of encouragement, followed by a nation, to the promised future (Josh. 1).

Sometimes your door opener turns out to be the last person you would expect. Esau was the last person Jacob ever thought would be his door opener. Jacob had dishonestly robbed him of his birthright and fled. Now, years later, he was returning home with the family God had blessed him with. His anticipation, however, was mixed with fear, fear of what Esau had every right to do to him, fear that he would never again walk through the doorway to home. As they entered the homeland, Jacob looked ahead and saw Esau approaching with 400 men. Was the older brother set on vengeance? Did he intend to get his rightful compensation, his personal justice, with a few quick slashes of the sword? Now Jacob was vulnerable, as he, Esau, had been vulnerable, first through hunger and then through absence, when the younger brother had robbed him of almost everything.

God was there that day, because, instead of slamming the door in Jacob's face forever, Esau opened it wide. "Esau ran to meet him, and embraced him, and fell on his neck and kissed him, and they wept" (Gen. 33:4).

They wept and they laughed as Jacob introduced all his family, and his children stared in wonder at their strange red-bearded uncle. Esau was embarrassed by the lovely gifts they gave him, but they insisted he keep them. Then Jacob said something quite amazing for a Hebrew to say: "Truly to see your face is like seeing the face of God" (v. 10). Esau defied human logic and legalism, put aside his own advantage, and became a face for God. And Jacob passed through the door opened, to the promise God had given. Door openers like Esau are able to transcend their own self-interest and open doors for others. If you look into the faces of your door openers, you might see the face of God as well.

I remember a community leader in Atlanta telling me about something that happened to her when she was a little girl. She came from a poor family. As part of a school research project, she decided that she wanted to interview the great journalist and newspaper editor Ralph McGill. To her surprise, he not only agreed to see her but, during that hour they spent together, treated her as if she were the most important person in the world. At the conclusion of the interview, McGill asked her a question that was to change her life: "And where will you be attending university when you're graduated from high school?" She had never before thought of university as a possibility for her future; people in her family had not had such opportunities. But when the great news-paperman put the question to her, he opened a door for her that she determined that day she would walk through. And she did.

Faces of God to Each Other

As you run down the playing field, moving toward your future in Christ, look around you. Look for the encouraging faces on the sidelines. Look for your supporters who are ready to run alongside you when you need them or to help you take a time-out to get yourself back together. Look ahead of you as well; you will see those who are clearing paths down which you were afraid you would never be able to go, helping you see plays that could break the game wide open. They are the outrageous door openers of our lives who dare to believe in us and think us to beyond where we think ourselves.

Life is not about winning and getting ahead. It's about finding your true humanity—your holiness—and living it. Your real encouragers are those who have in some way helped you do this, to be who God knows you are. They have also helped you to become an encourager of others. The greatest joy of encouragement, you discover, is the joy of giving it to someone else. Never are we more truly human, and rarely are we more holy.

12

Good Reason No. 5: Fruit of the Spirit

When all is said and done, for those who have cast their lot with Christ, joy is there for the taking, like ripe fruit on a tree. We know it can't be manufactured. It can be received only as a gift. Christ gives this gift to His Church like a generous farmer sharing an abundant harvest. In fact, the apostle Paul actually says that joy is included in the "fruit of the Spirit" (Gal. 5:22). In other words, joy is part of a harvest of which the Church has an endless supply. Christians have every good reason to enjoy life—and no reason to indulge in stern piety.

DULL SANCTIMONY AND HILARIOUS HOLINESS

But alas—there seems to be a persistent predilection for dull sanctimony pervading much of the Church. Peter Berger observes that the theologians, with notable exceptions, have shunned the idea of hilarious enjoyment having any importance in Christian experience. Greek Church Father John Chrysostom, for example, claimed that because there was no account in the Gospels of Jesus actually laughing, He never did. This conspiracy against laughter in the Church has, it seems, continued in one form or another throughout most of the last two millennia. As Berger observes, "There is a long line of grim theologians." Intellectual defenders of the faith have often considered it their duty to warn against laughter as a disapproved expression of sinful lightheartedness and even a lack of faith. Far better to weep over a lost, wretched world.

Fortunately, says Berger, the picture looks brighter when we turn from written theology and observe actual behavior. Medieval Christians, for example, developed a wonderful comic culture. One of the most intriguing manifestations of this was the so-called Easter laughter (*risus paschalis*). In the course of the Easter mass, the congregation was encouraged to laugh, to celebrate the joy of the Resurrection. Preachers would tell jokes and funny stories to elicit this laughter. In some places this practice continued into modern times.

Martin Luther, the great Protestant Reformer, was well known for his healthy sense of humor. As we enter the modern era, we happily meet some theologians who are prepared to reclaim humor as an important expression of Christian joy and Kingdom living. One modern martyr, Alfred Delp, a Roman Catholic priest executed by the Nazis, asked the chaplain who accompanied him to the gallows what the latest news from the front was and then said, "In a half hour I will know more than you!"—precisely the kind of joke the early martyrs were reputed to have cracked on the way to their deaths.[1]

There is, of course, a place in Christian experience for grieving over a world that's set on a course of self-destruction and over people who are demeaning themselves and others through their sin. The condition of the human race is cause for great concern, and Scriptures give the clear message that God himself grieves deeply over them (Gen. 6:6; Mark 3:5; Heb. 3:7-10). So should the Christian. But there's no scriptural basis for living in sadness due to the world's sad state. On the contrary, the Christian's deep concern for that state calls him or her all the more to live the hilarious Kingdom life and thereby demonstrate the life-giving alternative. In fact, to exile oneself to obstinate sadness is to deny confidence in the Good News and to flirt with sin. Somewhere I came across this statement from *The Shepherd,* written by second-century apostolic father Hermas:

Put away sorrow from thyself, for she is the sister of doubtful-mindedness. . . .

Clothe thyself with cheerfulness, which hath favor with God always. . . .

For every cheerful man worketh good, and thinketh good, and despiseth sadness; but the sad man is always committing sin.

JOY AS FRUIT BORNE

Joy is the fruit of a trusting soul who is so filled with the Spirit that he or she no longer tries to make life happen but lets God lead. This release from having to produce or prove, this escape from the condemnation of our own inadequacy, this surrender to the work that the Spirit of God does within us when we're receptive—this freedom in the Spirit—is enough to keep us laughing. There is a sanctified comic relief in being able to let go of our forced goodness and open up to His good grace. That's why the saints, holy as they are, have smiles on their faces.

Joy is indeed the mark of true saints, those who have given up on manufacturing their morality and instead have received the righteousness of God through faith (Rom. 1:16-17). These are people who have had holiness handed to them, not across some drab counter as wages sternly earned, but on an undeserved silver platter laden with fruit—the fruit of the Spirit.

The "fruit of the Spirit" (Gal. 5:22) is the intentional opposite of the "works of the flesh" (v. 19). Notice how different the two ideas of "fruit" and "works" are. "Works" are things we do on our own, things we initiate, carry out, impose: they are *ours*. "Fruit," on the other hand, is something that comes about through a natural process with which we cooperate: it is *God's*. You don't *make* fruit—you *bear* it; it's natural to you when the conditions are right or when the natural process is allowed to work. Whatever we try to do on our own, without God or contrary to the nature He gives us through His Spirit, are the works of the flesh, or the actions of pride and presumption. But whatever we allow God the Holy Spirit to do in our lives is the natural fruit of the *Spirit.*

We, all of us, make the decision as to whether or not to be trees bearing the fruit that is natural to God, whether or not to trust God to work His miracle in us. This is not a tough challenge for spiritual elites only. It's a surrender, a giving in to the life-giving Spirit.

Try seeing yourself as a tree ready to bear fruit. The fruit is the outcome that really matters in life. You, the tree, are sound because you have been made a new creation in Christ. All you need is the right nourishment. This is precisely what the Spirit provides. He enables you to grow and bear fruit. He nourishes you into fruitfulness.

SPIRIT AND FLESH

The Bible has a term for this state of spiritual health: *life in the Spirit*. Life in the Spirit is a tree being nourished by the Spirit and bearing the fruit of the Spirit. The opposite, life in the flesh, is a tree poisoned by pride and bearing nothing. The apostle Paul invites us to find life by living in the Spirit and to turn our backs on the death that results from the poison of the flesh (Rom. 8:5-13). What he means by "flesh" is not our physical bodies but rather a life centered on ourselves. To live "according to the flesh" or to be "in the flesh" is to live outside God and inside ourselves, to attempt the folly of a self-nourished tree, to choose death (v. 6). From such a life comes no fruit, only the unnatural works of the flesh, artificial fruit that's dead on the branches of our unnourished lives.

Life in the Spirit, however, is life centered on God, nourished by His Spirit and sweetened with the aroma of Christ (2 Cor. 2:14-15). It's as tasty and tantalizing as ripe fruit picked from the branches of a healthy tree. Taste it, and you savor joy.

But let's get down to the details. What exactly is the taste of the joy-fruit of the Spirit? What comprises the irresistible flavor of life in the Spirit?

THE TASTE OF ENCIRCLING PROVIDENCE

We spoke in chapter 9 of the Church as a people who know their inclusion in a gracious providence. Joy-filled Christians taste an encircling providence that secures them in a world that threatens life.

The story of the conversion of Ireland begun under Patrick in the fifth century is, among other things, the story of a horrible universe of peremptory fate transformed into the glowing realm of a loving providence. When Patrick came, the island imagination was dominated by the presence of gods who could destroy you and heroes who could terrify you. Patrick introduced a God who could love you—and did love you. He unleashed a revolution that did not stop until the fearsome gods were rendered powerless, consigned, claims Thomas Cahill, to rather insignificant places as "the comic gargoyles of medieval imagination."[2]

Not only did this Celtic Christian revolution begun under Patrick transform Ireland, but also it was the primary impetus in the conversion of England, Wales, Scotland, and much of the European continent following the collapse of the Roman Empire and the devastation of Christian-Classical civilization by the Germanic tribes. There were many reasons for the evangelical success of this vibrant Celtic mission, but among the most important was surely the Celtic missionaries' all-out belief in providence. They saw God as a Trinity intimately involved in human life, working for the good of His family on earth. They drew the unconverted to a Father who created and sustained them, a Son who redeemed and restored them, and a Spirit who sanctified and was present with them. They invited a world living in great fear to allow this Triune God to adopt them, dwell with them, and encircle them with His providential care—to transform their world into a place where God was at work for their good and their lives into a place for Him to fill with His goodness.

All Spirit-filled Christians enjoy the taste of divine benevolence. They rejoice not because the world has no threats, but because sin has no final success. This they know as well as they know the taste of their favorite fruit.

THE TASTE OF OVERWHELMING GENEROSITY

Joy-filled Christians taste something else: *a generosity that overwhelms them*. Life in the Spirit is like biting into that favorite fruit of yours just after it has been picked at peak ripeness and knowing that in the world of tastebuds, "it just doesn't get any better than this." The overwhelming flavor of life in the Spirit is an inescapable, extravagant generosity. We know that we're getting far better than we deserve.

Some would say to that, cynically, "I should be so fortunate!" Alas, very few today seem to think they're getting much more than they deserve. Michael Medved, a film critic and author, has written about what he calls "a national epidemic of whining" in America. He says that "our cry-baby culture is influencing the world and cultivates a great and overwhelming sense of self-pity." He lays the blame on our overindulgence, incessantly fed by the electronic media, and on "the inability to express gratitude."[3] The more we are indulged, the more we think we have coming—and inevitably, the less we're then satisfied with what we get. No wonder most people whine.

But what about Spirit-filled Christians who enjoy the fruit of the Spirit, the ever-present savor of joy? Do they whine? I imagine they do from time to time when, for some reason or another, they forget who they are and what they have. It happens to all of us, especially when we're caught off guard by an unfortunate turn of events or when someone treats us with insensitivity or disinterest—when the immediate pain of misfortune distracts us from the overwhelming reality of God's goodness. The honest psalmist says this barrenness of divine favor is like the dryness of the watercourses in the Negeb of arid south Palestine; it's enough to cause worry and make you wonder about God's generosity. We forget the truth of our good fortune because something or someone succeeds in turning us to what we aren't and what we don't have. Ungratefulness is one of the most insidious threats to Christian faith. It succeeds when the incidents of unfairness in one's life are piled up and become an exaggeration sufficient to cloud the face of divine benevolence. But when that face does appear, so does generosity, like delicious fruit for the taking—or, as the psalmist describes it, like the gushing water of the Negeb watercourses when the inevitable refreshing rains of providence come (126:4).

There may be a close etymological connection between one of the Greek words for "joy" (hilaros) and the word for "benevolence" or "generosity" (hileos).[4] There's certainly a connection in experience. Joy is the fruit of a life nurtured on God's abundant generosity. If you allow the goodness of God to creep into your life, if you dare to let Him show you favor, if you begin to accept His extravagant beneficence, then the real laughing begins. The laughing of old Sarah, who hears a far-fetched promise of offspring still not given after decades of trying, says in effect, "That'll be the day!" But even in the mild sarcasm there resides a glimmer of hope. She holds her belief in excruciating reserve, knowing that God has pulled some surprises in the past and may be up to it again. Laugh, Sarah—God has plenty of benevolence left, plenty of generosity with which to overwhelm us.

Those who live in the Spirit know this overwhelming feeling. The gospel is an unlimited giveaway, and kingdom of God living is sheer pleasure. Living in the Spirit is allowing ourselves to be overwhelmed with this generosity.

THE TASTE OF FREEDOM

What we find in this generosity is the beginning of true freedom. God is so generous that He's willing to cut us loose from anything that holds us in bondage. This bondage may be to the self-destructive behaviors of the body practiced by the overt sinner or to the more subtle, but no less insidious, self-destructive behaviors of the spirit practiced by the religious legalist. The message of the gospel is the astonishing claim that God in Christ releases us from these bondages. Wherever authentic religious revival has swept the Church, the truth of this claim has been proven again.

In the 16th century Martin Luther, along with many others, rediscovered a generous God ready to save a human race in shackles, ready to set them free and give them new life. It brought so much joy to his life that he could hardly control the excess of his language to describe it. The person graced by God, he said, now serves Him with "a hilarious and free will" (*hilari et libera voluntate*).

This, then, is the third thing joy-filled Christians taste: *a freedom that releases them.* Now it's more than being cut loose from a bondage. We're freed not to wander aimlessly, but to become who we are, sons and daughters of God. We're cut loose from the moorings that bind us in sin, not to become lost at sea and devoid of direction, but to find our true moorings, those that bind us to God while giving us plenty of rope—more than we'll ever need—to become who we are.

The paradox is that without being tied to the right moorings, there is no freedom. Most people are moored to something: it's to either what frees them or what enslaves them. I imagine it's theoretically possible to be completely adrift without any point of reference, any purpose, any allegiance, any hope. I can't imagine continuing very long, or surviving, in such a state. Most who are lost grasp at some mooring, at least for the time being, something that promises a measure of solace or immediate self-identity, perhaps a cure-all for the moment. But this is not home.

Home is where freedom is. Jesus said, "If the Son makes you free, you will be free indeed" (John 8:36). He had just been speaking of the son who, unlike the slave, had a permanent place in the household (v. 35). "The household of God" is the mooring for our lives, the place where we find family freedom, the true liberty of the sons and daughters of God. Here we serve God, not as a Taskmaster, but as a Father, and we do it with "a hilarious and free will."

The Taste of Play

If this sounds like fun, it is. In fact, the fruit of the Spirit comes with plenty of good fun. Joy-filled Christians have the taste of *a playfulness that distinguishes them.* Church is meant to be fun, filled with those who who have "chang[ed] and become like children" (Matt. 18:3), and if children are anything, they're playful.

I'm intrigued by the importance of children's play. Take away that play, and you probably destroy the children, or at least seriously damage their development. Their world of play is reality for them. It's a world in which they can be themselves and, in fact, develop themselves.[5] It's the training ground for their future, the world they create so that they can become the true persons they are.

I wonder if adults need play for the same reason, if they need to create playful spaces to help them keep in touch with reality, or at least to see and experience things from another perspective, or perhaps just to "be themselves." Our adult perceptions and behaviors are highly programmed, but play helps us to break out of the mold, to see things differently, to act outside expectations—to find an enjoyment outside the lines of our socially defined lives.

My wife, Keitha, knows how to play. She's forever stepping outside the lines and finding enjoyment in looking at things differently and uncovering humor in more things than you could imagine. Her laugh is one of her hallmarks; you can hear it from quite a distance. I remember one time when we were chatting with some folks following a Sunday morning service in Vienna, Austria, where we were living for a short time. The conversation touched on something that struck Keitha as funny, and she burst into her usual rollicking laughter. A retired minister came over to her and said sharply, "We don't laugh after the service." We were young then (it was the first year of our marriage) and assumed that Keitha had simply crossed over some line of customary behavior innocently. We now know that what she did was far worse: it was subversive—she was being playful in church. She was being herself.

I believe that Church was meant to be a playful place. By all rights and reasons, Christians should see more humor in life than anyone else. Like children entering their world of reality in play, Christians enter the world of the gospel and play it for real. Church is where they can reaffirm the reality of that world and better understand its disjunction with the spirit of the age. It's also where they can confess their own failures to live up to gospel reality. But they don't do it groveling—they do as affirmed sons and daughters. Church is for those who "play gospel" for all it's worth, trying their best to get it right in Church so that they can get it right the rest of the week. Church is child's play. The fruit of the Spirit is joy, because the Spirit helps us to become what Jesus invited us to become: believing children earnestly playing kingdom of God with all its outrageous unrules and holy humor.

What continues to surprise (or shock) people is that these believing children who insist on playing Kingdom are the true saints. The saints, by definition, are the Spirit-filled, fruit-bearing children of God. They are sanctified by grace, and for this reason they don't carry their holiness like heavy baggage to convince themselves or impress others. They carry it lightly like rollicking children, children who have entered a world gifted to them, squealing with delight as they savor the kingdom of God. They carry it like the taste of delicious fruit: not to be measured, only enjoyed.

The saints are those who live their Spirit-filled lives with the savor of encircling providence, overwhelming generosity, liberating freedom, and holy playfulness. They taste of joy. And like the psalmist they know that "light dawns for the righteous, and joy for the upright in heart" (97:11).

13

Good Reason No. 6: The Hilarious Fellowship

The Church is a fun-loving crowd. They enjoy being together with Jesus. As He put it, when the Bridegroom (Jesus himself) is present with the wedding party (His disciples), it's banqueting time (Luke 5:34).

DELIGHTFUL COMMUNITIES

Not surprisingly, the description we have of the very earliest Christian communities in Jerusalem resonates with good cheer. Try to feel the atmosphere:

> Awe came upon everyone, because many wonders and signs were being done by the apostles. All who believed were together and had all things in common; they would sell their possessions and goods and distribute the proceeds to all, as any had need. Day by day, as they spent much time together in the temple, they broke bread at home and ate their food with glad and generous hearts, praising God and having the goodwill of all the people. And day by day the Lord added to their number those who were being saved (*Acts 2:43-47*).

What jumps out at me from this description of how the early Christian community lived its life together is that *they lived it with delight!* They witnessed signs and wonders, they shared possessions, they spent time together, they broke bread together, they praised God—with delight! They delighted in good times; and even when they were persecuted, "They rejoiced that they were considered worthy to suffer dishonor for the sake of the name" (Acts 5:41). Nothing, and no one, could pry away their joy.

It was a joy they shared, a community joy. In chapter 6 we saw that joy becomes possible only in community: joy is the sign that the barrier of isolation has been broken and we have connected. There's nothing more depressing than being utterly alone; and there's nothing more delightful than being in fellowship with others.

The Bible fully understands the importance of one's life being shared in community. In fact, a thorough reading of the Bible makes quite clear that a shared life with other Christians is not an option for the believer—it's an imperative. *To be a Christian is to be called to fellowship.*

The apostle Paul says that "we, who are many, are one body in Christ, and individually we are members one of another" (Rom. 12:5). He tells the Gentiles, the once excluded, that now in Christ "you are no longer strangers and aliens, but you are citizens with the saints and also members of the household of God" (Eph. 2:19). The evangelist John explains that Caiaphas, the high priest, unwittingly prophesied that Jesus was about to die not only for the nation of Israel but also "to gather into one the dispersed children of God" (John 11:52). As sin broke community, so redemption restored it.

DIVIDING WALLS

The gospel's pull toward fellowship, however, is counterbalanced by a persistent pull toward partition. Robert Frost wrote a poem about walls we erect and maintain between us. He and his neighbor met every spring to mend the wall separating their property. But Frost kept wondering why the wall had to be kept in repair, since he had apple trees and his neighbor had pines. The neighbor only said, "Good fences make good neighbors."

It would be quite a different matter were there cows involved: cows roam and trespass. Frost said that before he would build a wall, he would like to know what he was walling in or out and who might be offended by the wall.

Why do we build walls? Certain walls are necessary. The

very skin on our bodies is a nice-fitting (well, for some of us!) elastic wall that keeps what's inside there and protects from dangerous intrusions from the outside. The basic need for shelter calls for some kind of barrier to protect us from the elements as well as gives us a degree of needed privacy. The earth's atmosphere, we're told by scientists, is a gaseous wall protecting us from life-threatening rays. These kinds of walls sustain life.

There are other kinds of walls whose purpose is far more complicated. Throughout Europe are ancient towns and fortresses surrounded by the remains of awesome barriers, painstakingly erected and usually effective in their day. What was the calculus by which it was determined who should be inside and who outside? And what about the Berlin Wall, which generated such euphoria in its breaking down? Did the builders of it really think it would keep freedom out and Communism safe?

Such walls, of course, are testimony to a human race who can no longer trust a neighbor, no longer risk vulnerability, no longer tolerate differences. They are the wraparounds of our enmity, the protection of our hatreds, the testimony to our sinful dividedness. They are the symbols of countless unseen walls, more powerful than the seen, precisely because they're harder to identify and easier to deny. "Now, I'm no racist," we insist while we do our best to protect our neighborhood from encroachment by persons of other races by quietly accepting and promoting unseen walls that make inclusion very difficult, if not impossible, for the outsider.

Our lives may be surrounded and even suffocated by a maze of invisible walls we can pretend we haven't built and don't hide behind. But the Scriptures are clear: they say that sin creates barriers between us.

Do you remember that Adam and Eve were given a wraparound wall of protection called "clothing"? They needed protection from their shame. It's interesting how this wall of protection has so often been used to intensify our divisiveness. Don't we sometimes dress competitively to outdress—and therefore socially subdue—others? We also dress in similar ways, not only to identify with our particular social group, but sometimes to make another group or person, who cannot or will not dress that way, feel excluded.

Can we possibly count all the ways in which we erect walls and nurture enmity between us?

CLOSED COMMUNITIES

If we based our conclusions purely on the weight of observable evidence, we would probably concede that it's the nature of communities not only to be exclusive toward those outside but also to break up into smaller communities of exclusion themselves or simply break down completely. Half of the marriages in the Western world don't hold together, and many of those that do remain intact carry the unhealed wounds of resentment and hurt, wounds that impair the health of what could be a deeply loving and satisfying relationship. The typical family seems soured by fallings out and unresolved anger. People have an uncanny capacity not to get along with some of their neighbors, employees with certain of their coworkers or perhaps their bosses. Though sometimes insisting that they want to "bring the community together," politicians often thrive on polarizing communities and mercilessly attacking their opponents because this is what they think works to their own advantage. Most nations are seriously divided over a wide array of issues, and those that are not are usually in the hands of a repressive government that gives no place to dissent; but remove the repressive force, and one quickly learns the measure of buried brokenness that rises to the surface when everything breaks loose. It seems to be the nature of communities to break, to prove themselves incapable of holding together well.

Philip Yancey gives us a test-tube example of this inclination:

I once shared a meal with two scientists who had just emerged from the glass-enclosed biosphere near Tucson, Arizona. Four men and four women had volunteered for the two-year isolation experiment. All were accomplished scientists, all had undergone psychological testing and preparation, and all had entered the biosphere fully briefed in the rigors they would face while sealed off from the outside world. The scientists told me that within a matter of months the eight "bionauts" had split into two groups of four, and during the final months of the experiment these two groups refused to speak to each other.[1]

Is this breaking of a community an unavoidable reality that we must learn to accept and find ways to cope with? Is it a "natural process" that we must simply minimize and manage as adroitly as possible so as to keep it from destroying us?

No Enemies

Or is it, as the Bible claims, a subversion of our true humanity, the opposite of genuine community—a distinctively unnatural condition and act bequeathed by our fallenness? Is it our inhumanity? The Church stands with the Bible and answers "yes." But it goes beyond this simple explanation of the problem and proclaims the arrival of the solution: the brokenness has been mended. In Christ we can be human again, we can dare to release our ruptured relationships for healing. The apostle Paul states the reason: "In Christ Jesus you who once were far off have been brought near by the blood of Christ" (Eph. 2:13). In other words, God really was in Christ reconciling us to himself (2 Cor. 5:18). If this is true, how can we be "friends of God," be called to make everyone else His friend, and still have enemies?

Every Christian has to grapple with the troublesome reality that in Christ he or she has no more enemies. When Jesus said, "Love your enemies," by simple logic He spoke a contradiction, a sentence that could not logically hold together: by definition you don't love your enemies—you hate them. To love them is to treat them as something other than your enemies, to refuse to validate their status as your enemies. When a church leader a few years ago publicly prayed for the nation his country had defeated in war, causing the prime minister, who was present, to take offense, he was acting under the compulsion of Christlike love. As a genuine Christian, he could do no other. The people of that nation were not his enemy.

Christ calls us to be a people who have given up having enemies. The Church is summoned to be the place where this calling is credibly demonstrated. Has the Church sometimes failed miserably in carrying out this calling? Yes. In fact, it has failed often. If the letters of Paul that are included in the New Testament are representative of how often he had to deal with failure to be reconciled to others within the congregation, this problem has clearly been with us from the beginning of the Church. With respect to the Ephesian churches, the apostle is clearly concerned about the long-standing division between Jew and Gentile, a division that clearly still exists within some of the congregations. He knows that this division, and any other, is a violation of the reality of Christ's reconciling work. So he restates the reality: "For [Christ] is our peace; in his flesh he has made both groups into one and has broken down the dividing wall, that is, the hostility between us. He has abolished the law with its commandments and ordinances, that he might create in himself one new humanity in the place of the two, thus making peace, and might reconcile both groups to God in one body through the cross, thus putting to death that hostility through it" (Eph. 2:14-16).

To give up all our enemies is to make ourselves completely vulnerable, as Jesus did. Enemies give us reason to protect ourselves, to hide (or deny) our weaknesses, to have some wall of safety to maintain. And behind that wall is someone who is not yet fully free (us).

But God is merciful even with His Church, and He waits, invitingly and patiently, as its members trip over remnants of "the dividing walls of hostility," come gradually to realize that divisions bring only harm and hurt, and hopefully move decisively toward the freedom of giving up all enemies. It's a letting go that's one of the most difficult actions of the soul set free. It requires a reckless trust in reconciliation.

LABORATORY OF RECONCILIATION

If the gospel is the good news that reconciliation has come in Christ, then the Church is the laboratory for proving it. As with all laboratories, it takes many attempts and much trial and error for individual laboratories (congregations) to get it right. Sadly, some never do. Perhaps they've not gotten the full message of reconciliation. Or perhaps they've not been willing to risk trusting the message completely and living without the self-protective luxury of enemies. But for those who want to get it right, the formula is quite simple, though tough to apply: risk living without enemies. In your own fumbling, stumbling way, treat your brothers and sisters in Christ as friends, and refuse to consider them as enemies.

Please note what treating them as friends really means. It doesn't mean that you let them walk all over you, but it does mean that you walk the way with them. It doesn't mean that you don't disagree with them, but it does mean that you speak your mind caringly, sensitively, and with all humility. It doesn't mean that you blame them for your own problems, but it does mean that in appropriate ways you trust them with your feelings, both positive and negative. It doesn't mean a showy friendliness that only postures, but it does mean a reliable friendship that puts itself on the line and survives the tougher tests. It means being what you are in Christ: a community, a we're-in-this-together-for-the-long-haul community, a friends-forever fellowship.

It's no accident that the word "saint" always appears in the plural—"saints"—in the New Testament. If you want to find a New Testament saint, you'll only find him or her in community. When we refer to someone as "a saint" in a way that suggests the person is one in and of himself or herself and in a way that distinguishes him or her from other Christians, we're going beyond biblical usage. The apostle Paul never distinguishes the readership of his letters to churches by saying, "To the church at (name of location), both the Christians who are saints and those who aren't." He throws the whole lot of them together and calls them *all* saints—even though he usually has to address the very unsaintly behavior of some in that fellowship later in the letter.

ALL BELONGING SAINTS

I think it's for good reason. In a circle of Christian friends we can't have saints and nonsaints. We can have only saints in various stages of becoming who they are in Christ. As a matter of fact, in a circle like this even the outsider who visits the group or is touched by the group in some way is not so much considered a nonsaint as he is an "about to be" saint. Recently I visited a new church that had a lively contemporary worship band. I had visited the church two or three times before, but this was the first time I had seen the middle-aged person who was playing drums. I learned that he had been invited to the church a few weeks before. When his skills as a drummer became known, he was further invited to play in the worship band. The member who was relating this to me then said, "He isn't a Christian, but he *will* be." I was struck by this positive way of seeing this person not as an outsider, but as an "about to be" saint.

The Church, then, is a fellowship of saints, those who are becoming and those who are being invited to. It's the place where everyone is invited to belong to "God's own people" (1 Pet. 2:9), the place where the gospel is proclaimed "so that you also may have fellowship with us" (1 John 1:3). It is the household of God, the home of all undeserving saints, the fellowship of grateful belongers.

THE CHARACTERISTICS OF A JOYFUL CHURCH

The all-pervasive character of the Christian fellowship is joy. Some outside observers at the first Christian Pentecost were so struck by the euphoria they witnessed that they were at a complete loss to explain it. Some jumped to an immediate conclusion: these people had been drinking far too much wine! (Acts 2:12-13). There were probably others who suspected temporary insanity. But Doris Donnelly is right: "Joy is not the sentiment of people who have lost their marbles and their hold on reality. Nor is it a pious wish, but rather a permanent, all-pervasive character of the Christian, irrepressibly active, filled with inward satisfaction and outgoing benediction." She goes on to say that "the early Christian communities understood themselves as post-Pentecost communities of joy, and anything that deflected that joy warranted a red-alert warning."[2]

That first Christian Pentecost community was neither an aberration nor a one-time phenomenon: it stamped the character of all future Christian communities. That's why the apostle Peter, representing the 12 apostles, it seems (Acts 2:14), interpreted what was taking place, not as something unexplainable or abnormal, but as "what was spoken through the prophet Joel" (v. 16), the sign that the messianic age had come. The Holy Spirit had been poured out on all flesh, and the Church were those who knew it and received Him. Nothing could be the same again. There was a new normalcy for a new Kingdom. There was a new joy for a new community.

A DEEP GRATITUDE FOR ONE ANOTHER

It is worth identifying some of the characteristics of this new community that were the keys to this otherwise unexplainable joy. The first characteristic was *a deep gratitude for one another.* It was almost as if some people were noticing one another for the first time and finding out how much joy they could bring to each other. Of course, they continued to have their squabbles, disagreements, and a few fallings out. Sometimes they rubbed each other the wrong way. But what carried them through all this was a new appreciation for one another, the Holy Spirit's gift of a new gratitude.

The best example of this gratitude is probably the apostle Paul. Again and again he confesses what a joy his churches are to him. These sometimes fickle fellowships, these congregations who could sometimes turn against him and cause him pain—*they* are his joy! Well, is it not true that those we love the most have the greatest capacity to make us unhappy, and sometimes exercise that capacity? But are they not also a source of deep joy? They may do things that bring us hurt, but they are too much a part of us not to bring a certain joy born of love.

Paul's congregations are his joy. He addresses the Philippian church as "my brothers and sisters, whom I love and long for, my joy and crown" (4:1), and he rejoices that they have "revived [their] concern for [him]" (v. 10). The Thessalonian Christians are his "glory and joy" (1 Thess. 2:20). "How can we thank God enough for you in return for all the joy that we feel before our God because of you?" he asks them (3:9). He tells the Roman congregation that he wants to come to them "with joy and be refreshed in [their] company" (Rom. 15:32). He even shares his joy with that troublesome Corinthian congregation because they have finally come around (2 Cor. 7:13), repented (v. 9), and now they are all able to share their joy together (2:3). With deep affection he says to them, "We are workers with you for your joy" (1:24). Paul's wish for them, and his work for them, was to the end that they might know the same joy to which his own life danced.

Within those same congregations there were individuals who seemed to be a special source of blessing and joy to the apostle. There was Philemon, to whom he writes, "I have indeed received much joy and encouragement from your love" (v. 7). And knowing what joy Epaphroditas could bring a saddened soul, he decides to share him with the Christians in Philippi so that they too "may rejoice at seeing him again" (Phil. 2:28).

The true Church brims with joy. Indeed, believers are grateful for many things, but gratitude for one another is a special gift.

In our fallenness we are robbed of our gratitude for one another. We become compulsively suspicious of each other. Dividing walls of hostility are erected, and underneath the surface of learned social graces, we become competitors, or even enemies. But the fellowship of the reconciled, of those who have given up having enemies, is comprised of changed people who begin seeing one another as if for the first time. With the new eyesight they have been given, they see friends to be grateful for, and they start allowing themselves to be grateful for them. It's a quite new and liberating agenda, and it brings immeasurable joy.

THE INCLUSION OF EVERYONE

The second thing about this unusual fellowship that gives cause for joy is its *disarming inclusiveness*. In chapter 7 we spoke of the gospel feast as a banquet open to everyone, which is a subversive metaphor in a fallen world more comfortable with exclusion. It's the tendency of communities to find ways to exclude or to break into incompatible pieces. We get hurt, get mad, get out, and get even.

Into this fallen milieu of brokenness comes the Christ, who refuses to accept and live by the logic of exclusion. "Love your enemies," He says, "and pray for those who persecute you" (Matt. 5:44). "If anyone strikes you on the right cheek, turn the other also; and if anyone wants to sue you and take your coat, give your cloak as well; and if anyone forces you to go one mile, go also the second mile" (vv. 39-41). "Forgive others their trespasses" (6:14). "Do not judge, so that you may not be judged" (7:1). These and other commands of Jesus are a thoroughly illogical ethic in a world locked into the logic of getting even. Jesus invites us to step outside the circle of justifiable exclusion and create circles of unexplainable inclusion. There is no "reason" to include in our circle those who hate us, abuse us, take advantage of us, manipulate us, wrong us, look down on us with condescension or up at us with envy and distrust. What Jesus says flies in the face of a world that tries to get by by balancing wrongs. An eye for an eye, a tooth for a tooth—it sounds very good as a principle of justice. As far as law and order are concerned, the logic is undeniable.

But in the world of human relationships, Jesus throws logic out the window and asks us to love those who don't deserve to be loved and include those who should be excluded. He knows something terrible about the logic that says, "Give that person what he deserves; keep him outside the circle of our fellowship and favor." The terrible thing Jesus knows is that wrongs committed against another are part of a cycle. Someone is wronged and responds, logically, by returning the wrong. (If for some reason the initial perpetrator is not available, the retribution is usually redirected toward a vicarious figure, complicating the issue considerably.) What then happens is that the one who receives the retribution becomes the one wronged and must seek his or her own retribution in turn. The cycle continues indefinitely— until someone decides to break it, until someone decides to stand with Jesus by relinquishing rights to personal retribution, surrendering the self-justifying pleasure of having enemies, and returning good for evil.

When we do this, we're exercising an extraordinary bravery in a world that sees bravery very differently. The common understanding of bravery requires the identification of an enemy, against whom one displays unusual courage. The Christian understanding of bravery requires the elimination of all enemies, and the willingness to take the consequences of blocking the cycle of retribution. As the life of Jesus clearly shows, such a person is likely to be hated and sometimes attacked by those who are unwilling or afraid to give up the desperate cycle. He or she is a holy misfit in a world adjusted to the customs and procedures of reprisal.

His or her bravery begins with a longing from deep within, the longing for community, which Christ has given him or her the hope to believe in again. This person is willing to stake his or her life on the reality of the new kingdom of God, the kingdom that refuses human enemies and invites everyone to friendship, willing to risk the outrageously inclusive behavior that models the future toward which God is leading us.

The prophet Zechariah had a vision of that future. One of the images of his vision was of people inviting one another to come and sit under each other's "vine and fig tree" (3:10). Sitting under one's vine and fig tree was a Hebrew image of peace and prosperity (1 Kings 4:25; Mic. 4:4), but Zechariah added the powerful theme of inclusiveness to the image. Genuine peace and prosperity would come when people opened the doors of their hospitality wide enough for everyone.

The Church has been called to do that, to extend grace to more and more people. When it's faithful to that calling it experiences the special joy that can be found only in open families, the joy of not having to keep anyone out, the joy of inclusiveness.

THE EXPERIENCE OF HEALING

Another joy-generating characteristic of this fellowship to which the Christian is called is that it's a place of *healing*. Our own experiences may well have proven that, indeed, "a cheerful heart is a good medicine, but a downcast spirit dries up the bones" (Prov. 17:22).

Peter Berger writes,

> There is . . . evidence to the effect that humor is related to physical health and that it helps individuals recover from physical illness. . . . Not all humor does. There is unhealthy laughter, presumably associated with socionegative humor. But positive, essentially harmless laughter appears to be health-inducing. Thus it was found that hospital patients recover faster if they can look at their situation with humor. . . . Also, humor facilitates the interaction between patients and hospital personnel, as well as relations between different echelons of the latter. Beyond that, humor has been deliberately used as a therapeutic tool, especially by psychotherapists. . . . The patient laughs and ipso facto gains new insight into his condition.[3]

If humor is an instrument of healing, then I suspect that the process is also reciprocal. There are few things that bring greater joy than the release from debilitating illness and the healing of a broken relationship. These are recoveries that best take place in a community formed by a healing, reconciling gospel. James urges those who are sick to call the elders, who represent the entire community of faith, for prayer, anointing, and confession (5:13-16). Paul urges Euodia and Syntyche to mend the difficulties in their relationship and "be of the same mind," and then he asks the entire Philippian congregation to "help these women" (Phil. 4:2-3). The Church is called to be a place of healing, and when it is, the mark of joy is unmistakable (v. 4).

TEARS TOGETHER

But the Church is also a place where people can feel free to *weep together,* and this characteristic—odd as this may sound—is another important key to the pervasive joy. Only the fellowship that weeps together can rejoice together (Rom. 12:15). Joy and weeping are not mutually exclusive experiences. When the Temple in Jerusalem was rededicated following the return of the exiles, some "wept with a loud voice when they saw this house, though many shouted aloud for joy, so that the people could not distinguish the sound of the joyful shout from the sound of the people's weeping" (Ezra 3:12-13).

It was a time to weep, and it was a time to rejoice, and there was no shame or embarrassment either way. Paul speaks of the persecuted Church "as sorrowful, yet always rejoicing" (2 Cor. 6:10). It is as if the bedrock of joy actually gives a greater freedom to weep because of the confidence that the joy cannot be uprooted. "Weeping may linger for the night, but joy comes with the morning" (Ps. 30:5).

I'm suspicious of congregations who seem to be convinced that they must rejoice nonstop, that they must not give any indication that they are not "happy in the Lord" all the time. They wear plastic smiles, force positive mental attitudes, and say "Praise the Lord!" like broken records. Their joy doesn't ring true. Perhaps what they need is a good cry—a really good cry. Perhaps they need to claim their own hurts, experience their own pain, and admit where they feel broken. Then they need to weep over it and let the healing begin. Maybe then they can begin to rejoice in a way that has the feel of authenticity.

Perhaps that's the strange wisdom behind these words from Ecclesiastes: "Sorrow is better than laughter, for by sadness of countenance the heart is made glad. The heart of the wise is in the house of mourning; but the heart of fools is in the house of mirth" (7:3-4).

There is a shallow mirth that nervously covers serious matters not honestly dealt with and sorrows too long denied. But there is also a truly joyful heart that knows how to weep.

Christians are called to be a people who can genuinely weep because they can face up to their sorrows and begin working through them. What helps them do it? They have plenty of friends in the fellowship who stand by them and share the sorrows. And they do the same for these friends.

PRAYER TOGETHER

The final characteristic of this fellowship that is a key to its pervasive joy is the practice of *praying together*. The apostle Paul speaks of "constantly praying with joy" in every one of his prayers for the Philippian church (1:4). Again and again we read of the Early Church sharing prayer together and emerging from those sessions, it seems, with renewed vigor and direction. After prayer and fasting, the church at Antioch laid hands on Barnabas and Saul and sent them off on the Church's first great missionary journey west, a journey that was to establish the first Christian beachheads outside Palestine and Syria (Acts 13:3). The disciples in Jerusalem experienced a deep awe as they enjoyed fellowship; learned, ate, and prayed together; and witnessed many "wonders and signs" (2:42-43). Awe is the feeling or attitude we have when we experience something or someone that's quite beyond the confines of the ordinary; it's the overwhelming experience of transcendence usually associated with prayer. Whereas awe has the element of profound reverence—a quite natural reaction in the presence of the divine—it also has a buoyancy about it that makes you feel that you're being transported to a sublime place where the joy is almost too much to bear.

It may well be true that there is a joy that can be known only in prayer. In the fourth century A.D., Evagrius of Pontus, who occupies a central place in the history of Christian spirituality, wrote, "Know this, that as we pray, the holy angels encourage us and stand at our sides, full of joy, and at the same time interceding on our behalf."[4]

This is an inviting picture that encourages us to relax in prayer, to feel comfortable in God's presence, and to enjoy the circle of His care. Paul suggests that we need not even worry about what we're going to say or ask in prayer: the Spirit himself knows our hearts and will intercede "with sighs too deep for words" (Rom. 8:26-27). He then goes on to make one of the most comforting statements in Scripture: "We know that all things work together for good for those who love God" (v. 28).

Prayer connects us with God at the deepest level and blesses us with the joy of His providence.

Such prayer is not so much private worship as it is corporate worship. If Christians are to "pray without ceasing" (1 Thess. 5:17), they are to do it as part of the community of saints whose prayers are continually being lifted to God, like perpetual incense from a permanent altar (Rev. 8:3-4). Christians never pray to God alone. Their prayers are part of an unending worldwide concert of prayer. Whether private or corporate, their prayer also causes them to notice one another more; they pray for one another (James 5:16). If prayer does not draw a community together, it can hardly claim to be genuine prayer. Christian prayer is always family prayer.

This is why it brings joy. When we pray, even in our darkest moments, our family is praying with us and for us, and the darkness begins to fade like the night when the rays of a rising sun start to penetrate the air. This is the Church—our grateful-for-one-another, inclusive, healing, weeping-together, rejoicing-together, praying-together family. It's this Church that by all rights, and for all these reasons, should appear foolish in a world driven by the logic of competition, exclusion, suspicion, individualism, and self-advancement-at-whatever-cost. It's this Church that has so much freedom to claim that if it did so, it would look out of control and dangerously joyful. It's this Church that has been given the grace and power to be a hilarious fellowship.

EXTRAORDINARY FELLOWSHIP

Almost 2,000 years ago God called a group of ordinary people to become an extraordinary fellowship. They were to be a living foretaste of the new Kingdom run by grace. They were to risk appearing foolish in a world too afraid to trust grace. They were to love one another and give up enmity. They were to practice the vulnerability of forgiveness.

What they discovered was that when they allowed themselves to live in this strange way, they were able to enjoy life—*really* enjoy life—and have an incredible amount of genuine fun, so much fun that they appeared drunk to those who did not yet understand what was going on. They were simply hilarious—not "drunk with wine . . . but . . . filled with the Spirit . . . singing and making melody to the Lord in [their] hearts, giving thanks to God the Father at all times and for everything in the name of [their] Lord Jesus Christ" (Eph. 5:18-20).

Hilarious behavior in the Church is not the practice of a few unbalanced oddballs. It is a norm for the fellowship of the forgiven, who have Jesus to be grateful for. Those who are members of the Body of Christ have every reason to laugh.

14
※

Good Reason No. 7: Sabbath Delight

I have a suspicion that Satan gets more worried when he sees God's people full of joy than he does when he sees them hard at work. If he can get the saints to lose their joy while working ever so hard and staying very busy, then he can find a promising foothold, perhaps even bring a downfall. His is the interfering voice we hear in the background as we feast at our Lord's table, enjoy the fellowship of His family, and have a good time. He whispers something like this: "OK—you've had your fun. But now it's time to get to work, time to get on with the task of being a serious disciple of your Lord, time to get on with holy living. The party's over."

Unfortunately, too many of us believe him. We become somber saints who worry about everything. And we forget the party. And joy fades.

MARK OF A DISCIPLE

Joy is not a momentary flash of something that's always beyond our grasp, teasing us, but never really taking us. The Scriptures tell us that joy is God's gift to the righteous. "Light dawns for the righteous, and joy for the upright in heart. Rejoice in the LORD, O you righteous, and give thanks to his holy name!" (Ps. 97:11-12).

Joy, in fact, is the mark of Jesus' disciples. You see this mark again and again in the Acts of the Apostles. Paul and Barnabas were in Antioch of Pisidia preaching the gospel, first to the Jews and then to the Gentiles. There were converts from both groups. But some of the powerful Jews opposed the gospel, swayed a number of the leading citizens, and the evangelists were run out of the city. How did the preachers react to such treatment? The account says simply this: "And the disciples were filled with joy and with the Holy Spirit" (Acts 13:52). Joy was their mark, their faithful companion in all circumstances; and perhaps more than anything, it was what attracted people to Christ.

THE LAUGHING GOD

Perhaps the place where this joy comes most clearly into focus and is most vividly expressed is worship. In order to appreciate it there, we have to remind ourselves that God is sometimes fun to be with! There is a *laughter with God*.

Religion and fun mix well, because God laughs. His Son, for example, invited people to have fun with His riddles. One day in the Temple He asked the people how the Messiah could be the son of David if David called him "my lord" (Ps. 110:1), which, of course, a father would never call a son. The people, as the record shows, were delighted at the humor (Mark 12:35-37). John Austin Baker comments on the "jokiness" of a few of the miracle stories of Jesus and wonders if Jesus was having "a bit of fun":

> Why scare the disciples out of their wits by walking past their boat on the Sea of Galilee in the middle of the night, when the poor devils were having hard enough work of it as it was? In all the versions of the feeding of the multitude, too, there is an undercurrent of something very like teasing in the way Jesus begins by puzzling his disciples, and a similar tone occurs in the story of the fish and the coin.[1]

LAUGHING SAINTS

I understand that poet W. H. Auden once proposed that the Church resurrect the medieval practice of "Carnival," a celebration that has declined into the debauchery of Mardi Gras. Carnival used to be mostly clean fun, an observance of our oddness through exaggeration and parody. People would dress up in strange outfits and celebrate the jokes of life. It was a time when taking oneself seriously was inappropriate. There would be plenty of time for seriousness: Lent was just around the corner. These were believers: they must have imagined that God was laughing with them.

The best way to have fun, of course, is not to have to plan for it or force it. One of the most serious and highly respected teachers of Wesleyan holiness, Samuel Logan Brengle, once said that the individual who is filled with the power of the Spirit will make people laugh: "He may say tremendously funny things. But he will not be doing it just to have a good time. It will come naturally. It will not be 'dragged in on all fours.'"[2]

The Gospel writers tell us that Jesus and His disciples were criticized for having a good time at social gatherings and banquets (Luke 5:33). Clearly, religious leaders were expected to maintain a serious demeanor at all times. Jesus suggested that His critics imagine themselves at a wedding feast and then decide on the proper behavior. It certainly was not mourning. What you need to understand, Jesus said, is that in reality the Bridegroom is here, the feast is on, the good times are rolling. There will be plenty of time in the future for spiritual sobriety.

Beware the party poopers of religion! They would have us to be always sober in spirit. And they're wrong. It may well be that "the one thing the devil cannot bear is laughter."[3] The psalmist rightly asks of God, "In Sheol who can give you praise?" (6:5). With characteristic insight, George MacDonald notes somewhere that "it is the heart that is not yet sure of God that is afraid to laugh in God's presence." We are not cowering slaves of a tight-faced Sovereign. We are laughers with God, living in the land of pure delight.

One of the things we can enjoy most is bringing delight to God. This, in fact, is what worship is. Isaiah says that God's people could be called "My [God's] Delight Is in Her" (Isa. 62:4). He is using the image of a marriage in which spouses love to bring pleasure to one another. The apostle Paul also uses the image of a marriage to describe the relationship of Christ to His Church (Eph. 5:32). Worship is the place where, in response to God's amazing goodness and love, we seek to bring Him delight, we act like the Bride of Christ who we are.

THE SABBATH

For the Old Testament Jew, the Sabbath was the day set

aside each week for rest and worship. There were two theological rationales for observing this day, which was very different from all the other days of the week. The first was that after six days of world creation, God himself rested on the seventh, the Sabbath (Gen. 2:2; Exod. 20:11). The Jews believed that we needed one day a week for not working, for being unproductive. If God needed a break from work, we certainly do. Besides, He commanded us to take the day off (20:8-10). Whatever Sabbath worship is, it is not work.

This brings us to the second rationale for observing the Sabbath: proper employment practice. Everyone was to be given the day off. It was a reminder that they were no longer slaves, but free people. The oppression of Egypt was behind them, the freedom of the Promised Land before them (Deut. 5:15). The Sabbath celebrated their God-given right: no one was allowed to make anyone else work on that day. It bound the community together in the enjoyment of their shared privilege as the people of God.

Evidently, God is delighted when we observe a Sabbath by getting a good rest and caring for one another's freedom. "A good rest" does not mean sleeping in, though getting a little more sleep on the Sabbath than one gets in a fast-paced workday is probably a good idea. The Sabbath is a day for self-care, not self-indulgence. "Caring for one another's freedom" does not mean staying away from one another. It means discovering what it is like to be free together. God is delighted when His people come together to be refreshed as persons and re-formed as a people.

WORSHIP

Worship, of course, is the focal point of the Sabbath. All that this day means comes together as the people of God gather to enjoy Him and one another, to rest in grace, to celebrate their freedom and praise the Freedom-Giver.

One of my minister friends reminds me that worship must be understood and practiced as an end in itself and not as a means to an end. The true effectiveness of worship cannot be measured by liturgical correctness, emotional peaks, or statistical outcomes. As far as its worship is concerned, the only important question a congregation should ask itself (my friend would say) is, Have we praised, enjoyed, heard, and given ourselves to God?

Actually, I basically agree with him. There's danger in manipulating our worship to satisfy our own personal or organizational agendas. On the other hand, I think we can expect that worship will have positive effects. For example, if worship is central to what it means to be truly human, one would expect that it would bring some observable enhancement to life.

POSITIVE EFFECTS

Let's consider one example. Previous studies of people recovering from illnesses found that those who prayed or were prayed for tended to recover more quickly. What a more recent study found is even more interesting with respect to Sabbath worship. It found that people who attended a religious service once a week and prayed or studied the Bible once a day were 40 percent less likely to have high blood pressure that those who did not go to church every week and who prayed and studied the Bible less. Yet another recent study found that monthly church visits improved the mental health of the elderly. It seems that going to church is healthful. David B. Larson of the National Institute for Healthcare Research draws this conclusion with respect to attending church worship: "There is something to the social part that is very important, and you don't get that sitting on your couch."[4]

Some worship services, of course, are dull and depressing. It's difficult to imagine how such services could improve health. Worshipers are encouraged to dwell on the dark side of their unworthiness and sin. They sing dirges, mourn their plight, and throw up sorrowful hands over an unheeding world.

While I agree that confession and intercession are essential parts of worship, they are misplaced outside the context of adoration and gratitude. The God we approach with our sin and our concerns is the God who loves us, welcomes us, and forgives us, the God in whom we delight. The psalmist invites us to worship, not with admonitions to solemnity, but with these words:

Make a joyful noise to the LORD, all the earth. Worship the LORD with gladness; come into his presence with singing. Know that the LORD is God. It is he that made us, and we are his; we are his people, and the sheep of his pasture. Enter his gates with thanksgiving, and his courts with praise. Give thanks to him, bless his name. For the LORD is good; his steadfast love endures forever, and his faithfulness to all generations (Ps. 100).

JOYFUL NOISES

If you want to find the Church at worship, think "Sabbath delight," and listen for *joyful noises*. Of course, not everyone would agree that joyful noises are a measurement of the authenticity of Sunday worship. I go along with them to a degree: the frenzy and frothiness of worship measure nothing as far as spiritual depth is concerned. In fact, it may suggest something counterfeit. Further, I think it's dangerous to prescribe the exact behavior one should manifest in order to express true joy in God's presence. But what I do know is that the noises of true worship—whatever the culture, liturgical tradition, style, or approved behavior of that worship—carry the unmistakable note of jubilation.

The Salvation Army, the church that nurtured me to faith and commissioned me for ministry, had a reputation for making a noise that was *too* joyful. In fact, it hit Victorian England like an ear-piercing uprising. Its strongest critics were from within the churches, and one of the most frequent accusations was aimed at the lusty singing, the loudness of brass bands with drums and cymbals, and dancing in the aisles. Evidently, whatever worship was supposed to be, it certainly was to be more serious than joyful. In characteristic prose, cofounder William Booth responded to his fellow churchmen:

> If when slaves find freedom, and tradesmen make fortunes, and kindred, or friends, or neighbours are delivered from some threatened calamity, it is allowable to go mad with joy and to express it by hiring music, and beating drums, and letting off fireworks, and shouting till hoarse, and everybody says that is all right, then by the same rule, if you please, and whether please or no, we are the slaves who now have our freedom, the people who have made our fortune, we are the men who have seen our our kindred and friends and neighbours saved from damnation; and therefore, we have a right to be merry.[5]

So bring on the music, please. Strike up the band. Let the praises roll. Sing and make music in your hearts. Make a joyful noise unto the Lord!

THE LANGUAGE OF GOD

Someone has said that the Church has to sing together to be who they are, and even that music is the language of God himself.[6] In *The Chronicles of Narnia,* C. S. Lewis goes so far as to portray creation being sung into existence by a majestic, open-mouthed Aslan (the Christ figure).[7] Could it be, then, that if music brought creation into being, it has a special place in helping us hear the creative Word of God? Does God sometimes sing himself to us?

In the Old Testament we find an account of the kings of Judah, Israel, and Edom summoning Elisha for a prophecy. They were in a mess: they were marching against Moab but could not find water for themselves or for their animals. The first thing the prophet did was to ask for a musician. "And then, while the musician was playing, the power of the Lord came on him. And he said, 'Thus says the LORD . . .'" (2 Kings 3:15-16).

Perhaps if we made more joyful noises, we would hear more prophecies from the Lord. We would certainly worship better. Music is delight, and the Sabbath is to be enjoyed. Eager for worship, the psalmist David says, "I was glad when they said to me, 'Let us go to the house of the LORD!'" (Ps. 122:1). The prophet Isaiah saw Sabbath observance as an opportunity for enjoying God: "If you call the sabbath a delight and the holy day of the LORD honorable; if you honor it, not going your own ways, serving your own interests, or pursuing your own affairs; then you shall take delight in the LORD, and I will make you ride upon the heights of the earth" (Isa. 58:13-14).

Delighting in the Sabbath is clearly a necessary part of taking it seriously. And evidently, it might even get you a "ride upon the heights of the earth"—whatever that is!

A THANKSGIVING FEAST

It's sometimes suggested that the ancient Hebrews approached their worship as cowering sinners who offered their appeasing sacrifices in great fear of what a holy God might inflict upon their unworthy persons. To be sure, there certainly were times when their deplorable faithlessness warranted dread about how God might respond, but their approach to worship was conceived, not as appeasing, but as delighting and enjoying God. The burnt offering of Lev. 1 was a sacrifice of praise, bringing pleasure to God in the form of a "pleasing odor" (vv. 9, 13, 17). The sacrifice of well-being described in chapter 3 was also a pleasing odor to the Lord (v. 16), and it involved a covenant meal in which the worshipers ate in God's presence and, in doing so, joyfully celebrated the privilege of their covenant relationship with God and reconfirmed their calling as His elect (Exod. 24:3-11; Deut. 12:5-18; 27:6-7). It was described as "rejoicing before the Lord" (Deut. 27:7).

Worship was enjoyment begun with thanksgiving. The psalmist says he will offer his sacrifices "with shouts of joy," singing and making melody to the Lord (27:6). Another psalmist invites the pilgrims traveling to Jerusalem for worship to be prepared to "offer thanksgiving sacrifices, and tell of his deeds with songs of joy" (107:22). As with all forms of lasting enjoyment, worship as well begins with gratitude.

It was gratitude that overwhelmed the disciples of Jesus when in their despair they had been brought face-to-face with a resurrected Lord and He had communion with them over a meal, explained the events that had only perplexed them to that point, gave them the blessing of his peace, and commissioned them as His witnesses. In the last two verses of his Gospel, Luke tells us that then "they worshiped him, and returned to Jerusalem with great joy; and they were continually in the temple blessing God" (24:52-53). He concludes his Gospel with worship born of gratitude and overflowing with joy.

In the same vein, the apostle Paul admonishes the Ephesian church, "Be filled with the Spirit, as you sing psalms and hymns and spiritual songs among yourselves, singing and making melody to the Lord in your hearts, giving thanks to God the Father at all times and for everything in the name of our Lord Jesus Christ" (Eph. 5:18-20).

PURE AND PERFECT JOY

Worship is where we focus the daily gratitude of our hearts and find the deepest pleasure. To be sure, it's also where we hear the Word of God and sometimes come under its judgment and redirection; but everything that takes place in worship is part of the texture of gratitude and joy, and this fabric surrounds and secures the whole.

Simone Weil, in great pain from chronic headaches and spiritual turmoil, attended a worship service in the Benedictine abbey of Solesmes in northeast France. It was an experience of total surprise and led to her conversion. In her own words, it enabled her to "get a better understanding of the possibility of loving divine love in the midst of affliction." She described it simply as "pure and perfect joy."[8]

Weil would probably never have been at home where the joyful noises of worship reached a high decibel level. She was a philosopher at greatest ease with intellectual reflection and spiritual contemplation—and, of course, she had those headaches. But something inside her started to dance that day in the abbey worship, and in the integrity of her natural quietness, she started composing her own joyful noises heard around the world through her writings. Her worship, also, was sheer joy.

REHEARSAL FOR ETERNITY

There's a final secret behind the delight of worship. Worship is a drama being played out; or more accurately, it's a rehearsal— *a rehearsal for eternity.* When God's people come together for worship, they're letting eternity touch them, they are releasing themselves to the ecstasy of Christ's Lordship and the dance of His kingdom. William Willimon puts it this way: "Worship is a way of being in love, of glorifying and enjoying the One of whom we can say, 'We love, because he first loved us' (1 John 4:19)."[9]

Worship is the act by which God's people intentionally carve out a space for eternity and allow themselves to live for a time in that space. Here they let God love, claim, and redirect them, and they respond with their love and commitment. This drama prepares them for both the everyday and the eternal. It becomes the blueprint for everyday living. Life begins to look more and more like worship as worship merges with life.

Worship also becomes a foretaste of our future with God, a space in time with the character of eternity. The early Salvationists used to sing a chorus that began, "Every day will be Sunday by and by!" They were not thinking of a daily somber sacredness; they were anticipating daily Sabbath delight. Sunday meeting was the foretaste of a delicious eternity. Theologian Wolfhart

Pannenberg speaks of worship as the joyful anticipation of the celebration of God's glory, which will be consummated in the renewal of all creation in the new Jerusalem. This fact, he says, should certainly allow for "the element of play" in our worship.[10] Let the fun begin!

Like the Old Testament Jew who suspended all mourning when he came to Sabbath worship, the Christian comes to Sunday worship with a joyful heart, ready to dance to the music of eternity. The prophet Isaiah invited an exiled Judah to "sing to the LORD a new song" in anticipation of their restoration (42:10). The Church also sings a new song, in praise of their restoration in Christ and in preparation for their future with Christ. Christians come to worship like children experiencing something for the first time, laughing at the wonder and goodness of the songs they hear, the Word they receive, and the hope they're given. Unless you become as a child, you can't genuinely worship.

To worship is to break the bondage of our idolatrous mindset and to live by seeing and hearing God. In order to do this, we must do what God did on the seventh day of creation: rest. Much work may—and should—go into preparation for Sunday worship, but when worship begins, work is over. It's over in the sense that worship frees us from our obsession with our productivity, self-advancement, and temporal security, bringing us into the stream of effortless praise and providential trust. To worship is to step into eternity and enjoy God.

A SUBVERSIVE ACT

The irony of it is that this is the farthest thing from what it may seem on the surface: it is not escapism. It is the experience by which ordinary human beings are transformed into radicals. Worship makes saints, persons who regularly rehearse for eternity and reenter the day dazzled by God and captivated by the Kingdom that shapes eternity, persons purified by gospel light and cleansed by healing streams. By all rights, worship is a dangerous enterprise, because it nurtures radical saints transformed by eternity, and now they inflict themselves upon the world and work their subversion wherever they can.

If someone ever wanted to weaken Christian subversion in the world, a good place to start would be to water down its worship: take away the openness to God, the gratitude, the joy, the singing and dancing, the release from all things repressive, the honesty. Make worship proper, prescribed, and pathological. This would greatly reduce the possibility of saints emerging and would instead deliver Christians with no confidence in their freedom in Christ and their power to transform the world. They would be guilt-ridden and fearful of acting decisively. They might behave well, but they would not be very good saints.

True worship, however, is dangerous because it nurtures saints—hilarious saints, saints who are the most revolutionary inhabitants of the planet because they have sung God's songs and danced to the rhythms of His new creation. This is more than enough to worry Satan, and more than enough to begin putting the world right side up.

A Final Word
The Last Laugh

The saints are those who live well with God. They take God as He is. Not only do they serve Him, but they enjoy Him as well. They join in His laughter.

You and I are called to be saints. It is a call from which no Christian is excepted. It is the way we were meant to travel, the life we were meant to live, a life lived in the company of God.

It is a life of holy hilarity.

We pass up this joy at our peril, but unfortunately we are sorely tempted to do so. The grace-permeated, unshakable mirth of the saints is a threat to the self-centered happiness to which the insidious sinner in us aspires. The lure away from laughter is powerful.

Umberto Eco's novel *The Name of the Rose*[1] gives fascinating insight into this dilemma. It is about a series of mysterious murders in a monastery in northern Italy. As it turns out, the murders were committed by a monk who feared the discovery and spread of an old manuscript that he considered heretical. The monks he murdered were those who stood in the way of the manuscript's continuing secrecy.

What dangerous message did the manuscript carry? In the mind of the murderer, a deeply devoted cleric, the danger lay in its praise of folly, its elevation of laughter to a high place in theology, its celebration of joy as essential to genuine spirituality. The monk was quite content to give folly a secondary place as a means to "let off steam" and temporarily acquiesce to the average person's lower nature. But he was horrified at the prospect of hilarity inhabiting the core of human spirituality. Holiness had to be motivated by fear; saints had to be kept in line. Only repression could defeat the persistent strategies of the flesh. Hilarity could turn this kind of controlled holy living on its head; it was a menace.

When such a view prevails, joy becomes a dangerous emotion, a threat to the divine order of redemption, and stamping it out is required of all keepers of this order. In my view, the most insightful achievement of Eco's novel is its convincing portrayal both of the kind of threat to a power-based system that real joy poses and of the inevitable extermination efforts of those who have fully aligned themselves with that system, be it secular or religious. Joy threatens all forms of oppression. Saints like Francis of Assisi expose the idolatries of a civilization's order by seeing (and mocking) the false artifices of both power-focused organizations and repressive theologies. They do it with a new vision, by teaching people to "look at things from another direction" and to let themselves laugh at the foolishness they see, including their own. We would teach people to look at the world through the lens of the kingdom of God—to see like saints.

The Church, unfortunately, has participated in hilarity's murder. It has too often seen laughter as inappropriate to Christian behavior: Christians were expected, rather, to weep over a lost world. How *could* we laugh (so went the argument) when the world was in such a sad state and when we needed to be serious about the business of saving it?

In reality, we have every reason to laugh, and the dour world certainly needs a laugh. Perhaps our most potent weapon for saving it is the laughter of God, the laughter of the new Kingdom, the laughter that we, in our best evangelism, invite the world to join in, the laughter of death defeated and resurrection begun. Maybe the searching world does not want our sour seriousness. Maybe what it wants is our joy. Maybe it wants to be able to laugh again.

The gospel invites whoever is ready to start laughing: laugh over the sealed end of every kingdom of darkness. Laugh over the puniness of power in the presence of love. Laugh over a God who keeps popping up like a jack-in-the-box, inconveniently and unpredictably. Laugh over the surprise outcomes of prayer. Laugh over wisdom proven to be foolishness, and foolishness proven to be wisdom. And especially, laugh over sinners becoming saints.

Nothing could be more hilarious than that: sinners, both desperate prodigals and arrogant Pharisees, suddenly acting like saints, as if they were in the image of God. Such transformations first take one's breath away. Then comes the side-splitting part. This new holiness defies the predictability of a sinful course. The expected disastrous outcomes are overturned, the predicted failures proven wrong, and those with eyes to see miracles as the unexplainable surprises they are can't help breaking out into the laughter of the redeemed. Holiness breeds hilarity.

The saints find themselves laughing again and again, from here to eternity. With heads turned up in gratitude, they sing, "You show me the path of life. In your presence there is fullness of joy; in your right hand are pleasures forevermore" (Ps. 16:11).

Thanks be to God!

Notes

INTRODUCTION

1. I should point out at the beginning my belief that the people of God are called to live holy lives. A clear reading of the Scriptures draws us like a magnet to this truth. In the Old Testament, the chosen people of God are told that their character is holiness (Lev. 11:44-45). In the New Testament, the followers of Christ are told the same (1 Pet. 1:15-16). In fact, the apostle Paul asserts that Christ gave His life on the Cross "so as to present you holy and blameless and irreproachable before him" (Col. 1:22). It is my firm belief that this holiness is more than a declared state, a "position" that the believer has before God because Christ declares him or her righteous. It's also a call, a summons to participate in a new life, to adopt the lifestyle of a radically new Kingdom, to become a new person. I'm therefore unwilling to discount the call of all Christ's followers to holiness. It's there in the Book, and no rationalizing, no historical contextualizing, and no other means of explaining away can, with integrity, remove it. The truth of W. E. Sangster's statement still holds true: the Church is not despised because it is holy; it is despised because it is not holy enough. The call to holiness is not negotiable. In this book we'll explore the hilarious side of the life to which this holy calling leads us.

2. "Hilarity" may seem to be a rather extreme word. We typically use it to denote times of mirth and merriment when things are a bit, well, out of control. You would not be surprised to witness polite laughter at a state dinner, for example, but hilarity at such an event might shock you. As for suitable Christian conduct, you might say that joy is indeed a fruit of the Spirit, but so is self-control (Gal. 5:22-23). The word "hilarity" is derived from similar words that occur in both the Greek of the first century A.D. and the Latin of Early Church writings. The basic meaning is cheerfulness, goodness, or graciousness. The apostle Paul tells the Corinthian Christians that "God loves a cheerful [hilaron] giver" (2 Cor. 9:7). He urges the Christians in Rome who have the gift of compassion to exercise the gift "in cheerfulness [hilaroteti]" (Rom. 12:8). The far more common words used in the New Testament to denote the joyful dimension of Christian living are xara (joy, joyfulness, festiveness) and xairo (to rejoice, be glad). These two words appear again and again, and it would be fair to say that without them and without the buoyancy and vigor they bring to the message, the New Testament would be an entirely different book. In fact, I would argue that if you removed joy from the way of life the New Testament is trying to sketch out for us, you would have rendered that life meaningless. The way of life that Jesus and the Early Church taught and lived is incomprehensible without joy.

CHAPTER 1

1. "The threesome God," of course, is one way of describing the Trinity, a doctrine that's central to Christian faith. Christians believe in the one God who is also Three. The three Persons—Father, Son, and Holy Spirit—are actually one, that is, sharing the same being and also living in perfect harmony and relationship with one another. Nevertheless, the One is still Three. In a very real sense, God is in community with himself; He is, and has always been, in relationship, even before He created other beings to whom He could relate. This is why God is fun-loving. An "unmoved Mover," a God of the kind of perfection that allows no diversity, a God who is One but not Three, is without humor. How can you have fun when you're utterly alone?

2. Robert C. Morris, "God at Play in the World," *Weavings,* November-December 1994, 7.

3. See Walter Brueggemann, *The Message of the Psalms* (Minneapolis: Augsburg Publishing House, 1984), 38-39.

CHAPTER 2

1. James H. Rutz, *The Open Church* (Auburn, Maine: SeedSowers, 1992), 57.

CHAPTER 3

1. Quoted in Donald E. Demaray, "The Merits of a Merry Heart," *The War Cry,* U.S.A. edition, October 1996, 17.

2. Christian theology has a term for this: prevenient grace, the grace that "goes before" saving grace, preparing us and making it possible for us to respond to the gospel. The seeker's capacity for laughter, then, is a preparation for the joy that the gospel always brings, and his or her experiences of laughter are always practice runs.

3. Chapter 5 will deal further with the subject of humor without God.

4. Frederick Buechner, *Telling the Truth* (San Francisco: Harper San Francisco, 1977), 61.

5. I'm grateful to William H. Willimon for helping me see the humorous effect this story would have had on Jesus' hearers. (William H. Willimon, *With Glad and Generous Hearts: A Personal Look at Sunday Worship* [Nashville: Upper Room, 1986], 135-36.)

6. The publicans mentioned in the Gospels were collaborators with Rome, often Jews, who collected the imperial taxes for Rome, usually adding an exorbitant personal surcharge. They were despised by devout Jews, for whom the term "publican" was synonymous with the worst sort of sinner.

CHAPTER 4

1. See J. G. Ballard, "Is There Anybody Out There?" review of Timothy Ferris, *The Whole Shebang: A State of the Universe(s) Report,* in *London Sunday Times,* September 21, 1997, p. 8, Col. 6.

2. Annie Dillard, *Pilgrim at Tinker Creek* (New York: Harper and Row, 1974), 137.

3. See *The Interpreter's Dictionary of the Bible,* ed. George Arthur Buttrick (New York: Abingdon Press, 1962), 2:21-22, entry titled "ecstasy."

4. Emil Brunner, *Our Faith,* trans. John W. Rilling (New York: Charles Scribner's Sons, n.d.), 18. (Original German edition published in 1936.)

CHAPTER 5

1. Cited in Richard Adeney, *Strange Virtues: Ethics in Multicultural World* (Downer's Grove, Ill.: InterVarsity Press, 1995), n. 6, 272.

2. William James, *The Varieties of Religious Experience: A Study in Human Nature* (New York: Random House, 1902), 77.

3. Tom Sine has warned of the merging of "the American Dream," which is the pot of gold at the end of the rainbow of happiness that Americans are supposed to have the inalienable right to pursue, and the Christian gospel. Many American Christians, it seems, equate the extent of God's work in their lives with the extent of their personal happiness. They "have unwittingly borrowed the life goal of a non-Christian religion [the religion of the American Dream] and made it central to their Christian faith." God is seen as the guarantor of one's personal happiness, the satisfier of one's selfish aspirations. (Tom Sine, *The Mustard Seed Conspiracy* [Waco, Tex.: Word Books, 1981], 73-86.)

4. Quoted in Michael Skube, "Life, Not Death, Provides Our Agony," *Atlanta Journal/Constitution,* December 26, 1993, sec. K, p. 8.

5. Paul Brand with Philip Yancey, "And God Created Pain," *Christianity Today,* January 10, 1994, 19.

6. The "altars" and "pillars" referred to constructions of Canaanite worship and therefore to Israel's apostasy, their abandonment of the true God, and their forgetfulness of their history with Him.

CHAPTER 6

1. Robert Nesbit, *The Quest for Community* (London: Oxford University Press, 1953).

2. Henri Nouwen, *Our Greatest Gift: A Meditation on Dying and Caring* (San Francisco: HarperCollins, 1994), 23 ff.

3. From "Bradenton Battlelines," newsletter of the Bradenton, Florida, Corps of The Salvation Army. Used by permission.

4. George Bernard Shaw, preface to *Major Barbara* (Baltimore: Penguin Books, 1951), 29.

CHAPTER 7

1. *The New Oxford Book of Christian Verse,* ed. Donald Davie (Oxford: Oxford University Press, 1981), 81.

2. Quoted in Thomas Cahill, *How the Irish Saved Civilization: The Untold Story of Ireland's Heroic Role from the Fall of Rome to the Rise of Medieval Europe* (London: Hodder and Stoughton, 1995), 174-75. From *Celtic Fire,* by Robert Van de Weyer. Copyright © 1990 by Robert Van de Weyer. Used by permission of Doubleday, a division of Random House, Inc.

CHAPTER 11

1. Recounted in Laurie Beth Jones, *The Path: Creating Your Mission Statement for Work and for Life* (New York: Hyperion, 1996), 38.

CHAPTER 12

1. Peter L. Berger, *Redeeming Laughter: The Comic Dimension of Human Experience* (Berlin: Walter de Gruyter, 1997), 197-203.

2. Cahill, *How the Irish Saved Civilization,* 149.

3. Quoted in Ray Simpson, *Celtic Daily Light: A Spiritual Journey Through the Year* (London: Hodder and Stoughton, 1997), June 28 devotional.

4. See *Theological Dictionary of the New Testament,* ed. Gerhard Kittel, trans. Geoffrey W. Bromiley (Grand Rapids: William B. Eerdmans, 1965), 3:298.

5. I found it interesting that in her book on personal mission statements *(The Path),* Laurie Beth Jones suggests that in trying to decide what your mission in life is, one of the important places to look is what you played at and how you played as a child (p. 43). If this is good advice, then a child's play is crucial for his or her development: what the child is at play holds a key to what he or she is meant to become, and the better the child plays, the more likely he or she is to be on the track of his or her mission as an adult.

CHAPTER 13

1. Philip Yancey, *What's So Amazing About Grace?* (Grand Rapids: Zondervan Publishing House, 1997), 83.

2. Doris Donnelly, "Good Tidings of Great Joy," *Weavings,* November-December 1993, 10.

3. Berger, *Redeeming Laughter,* 9.

4. Quoted in Simpson, *Celtic Daily Light,* October 3 devotional.

CHAPTER 14

1. John Austin Baker, *The Faith of a Christian* (London: Darton, Longman and Todd, 1996), 56-57.

2. Quoted by Peter Farthing,"The Leakage of Spiritual Power," *The Officer,* June 1997, 47.

3. Cahill, *How the Irish Saved Civilization,* 149.

4. Quoted in Robert Davis, "Prayer Can Lower Blood Pressure," *USA Today,* August 12, 1998.

5. William Booth, *Salvation Soldiery* (London: The Salvation Army, 1889), 118-19.

6. Patrick Henry, "Singing the Faith Together," *Christian Century,* May 21-25, 1997, 500-501.

7. C. S. Lewis, *The Magician's Nephew* (New York: Harper Collins, 1995), 104.

8. David McLellan, *Simone Weil, Utopian Pessimist* (London: Macmillan, 1991), 136-38.

9. Willimon, *With Glad and Generous Hearts,* 63.

10. Wolfhart Pannenberg, *Christian Spirituality and the Sacramental Community* (London: Darton, Longman and Todd, 1983), 36, 49.

A FINAL WORD: THE LAST LAUGH

1. Umberto Eco, *The Name of the Rose,* trans. William Weaver (New York: Harcourt Brace & Co., 1984).